B

Tomáš Šalamon received his master's degrees in computer science and finance from the Faculty of Informatics and Statistics and Faculty of Finance and Accounting at the University of Economics in Prague and his MBA from Kellstadt Graduate School of Business, DePaul University in Chicago. He earned his PhD from the Faculty of Informatics and Statistics at the University of Economics in Prague where he also teaches undergraduate and graduate courses. Topics of his lectures are related to this book. Among other areas he is interested in simulations of systems, multi-agent systems, data modeling and economic simulation. Besides his academic career he has managerial experience in several industries and is active in the local community.

Design of Agent-Based Models

Developing Computer Simulations for a Better Understanding of Social Processes

by Tomáš Šalamon, Ph.D.

ʹB

2011

Published in the Czech Republic by Tomáš Bruckner, Řepín – Živonín, 2011
Academic Series

This monograph is based on author's PhD theses Development of Agent-based Models for Economic Simulation.
The work was reviewed by Petr Hřebejk, Oracle Corporation, and prof. Jaroslav Král, Faculty of Mathematics and Physics, Charles University, Prague.

Paperback printed on demand and worldwide distributed by Lightning Source UK Ltd. Pitfield UK and Lightning Source Inc. La Vergne TN US. New prints are available for ordering in every bookstore.

Visit us at http://pub.bruckner.cz

ISBN 978-80-904661-1-1 (paperback, POD, worldwide market)

Dedication

Dedicated in loving memory of my mom.

Contents

CONTENTS

Introduction

The idea of multi-agent systems as a new paradigm of information systems' architecture appeared a couple of decades ago; since then it has been utilized for numerous purposes in the field of robotics, artificial intelligence, distributed information systems and many others. The unique features of multi-agent systems, such as distributedness, redundancy, robustness, and artificial learning, make it an interesting substitute for traditional software systems in certain application domains. The body of publications regarding multi-agent systems is huge and ever-growing in recent years. This book addresses one particular chapter of the big multi-agent story: agent-based modeling.

Agent-based modeling is a modeling and simulation method where multi-agent systems are used for the representation of social, economic, ecological and other similar systems in a software environment. Multi-agent systems can be very useful for this purpose due to their principal similarities with certain traits of human societies and natural ecosystems. Agent-based simulation can mimic such a society and allow us to perform tests, experiments and forecasts that would not be otherwise possible.

The method is however challenging for several reasons. Due to its strong interdisciplinary character, it needs a combination of knowledge from a number of sources, including economics, statistics and the development of information systems. Further, issues regarding multi-agent systems are discussed increasingly in recent years from various viewpoints, and the field offers a lot of open issues that ought to be solved.

Agent-based modeling appears to be a promising technology that has the potential to improve the modeling, forecasting, and experimental abilities in economics, finance and other social sciences and to overcome some drawbacks of the present methods. It may seem that scientific implementations and publications of the method are relatively abundant; however, after a deeper exploration we find that there is a lack of practical applications and a very low awareness of the method in the scientific community. Therefore a reader can easily find numerous resources about the theory of multi-agent systems and agent-based simulations; however, if he or she needs to find out how to develop such a system, the offering is much narrower. This book aims to help fill this gap and to answer the questions that can emerge when we are involved in the construction of agent-based simulations.

This book was written for both beginners and more advanced readers. It can provide basic insight into the fundamentals of multi-agent systems to the novices in this field, describing the various approaches to the development of multi-agent systems and making familiar the common terms and principles. As multi-agent systems are often treated as a subfield of artificial intelligence, many other comparable texts are hard to digest for beginners, as they are full of equations and logical formulae. The idea behind this book was to make the multi-agent systems and agent-based simulations comprehensible and accessible for more people, and that is why we build on practical examples and strive to explain the principles in as understandable a way as possible. For this reason also we have used it successfully as a textbook for students of computer science.

On the other hand, even advanced users can find this book valuable. A substantial portion of the text is devoted to the principles and procedures of the development of agent-based simulations. A methodology of agent-based simulations development is still an open issue, because most existing methodologies in this field are too general to become a useful tool for practical development of agent-based simulations. Readers who are already familiar with the theoretical foundation and who want to develop their own agent-based simulations often discover that they are really unsure where to start, what to do next and what to avoid, and so they usually have to proceed by trial and error. In order to avoid repeating the mistakes that others have already made, a methodology for the development of agent-based simulations could be very useful. This book presents the methodology called *Agentology*, which was developed on the basis of best practices for engineering of agent-based simulations and tested on several projects of various scale. The methodology is described step by step in a very clear form with many examples; its purpose is to be helpful for the practical development of agent-based simulations.

The structure of the book is as follows: in the first chapter, the existing methods of simulation in economics and other social sciences will be evaluated. There will be described discrete event simulations, system dynamics, various hybrid methods, participatory simulations and agent-based models.

The next part of the book will be devoted to multi-agent systems and their principles. We will discuss how the agents operate in various environments which we can divide according to a number of traits. Agents can perceive their environment, can take actions towards it and towards other agents, and can communicate with other agents. We will see that there are various approaches to agency that differ in their basic principles. The most important are reactive agents, deliberative agents and hybrid agents, and we will compare pros and cons of these individual concepts.

Perhaps even more important in multi-agent systems than the agents alone are their interactions, because they originate in the emergent properties of the system. We will examine different kinds of agent interaction in the fourth chapter.

After the exploration of theoretical principles of multi-agent systems, we will focus on the question of how these systems are actually being developed. Agent-oriented programming is a common term, but without clear content. Various authors have their own concepts.

In the next chapter, the existing agent methodologies will be assessed. We will discover that there is no wide selection of viable methodologies for agent-based modeling.

Although agent-based modeling is an interesting technology, we should not overlook its substantial drawbacks and limitations. Hence the next chapter will be devoted to their evaluation.

The last part of the book contains the description of the methodology called *Agentology*, which is intended for the development of agent-based models. As we will see, the methodology defines six roles of participation in the project, while the development process consists of four phases and nine steps (some of them mandatory; others can be skipped or reduced). For conceptual analysis the methodology offers a graphical modeling language, with a set of diagrams which will be presented in the last chapter.

Welcome to the wonderful world of agents!

Chapter 1
Methodology of social sciences

Social sciences (and particularly economics) traditionally use two main approaches to research: deductive and inductive. Researchers use deduction to form theorems and hypotheses on the basis of assumptions and then eventually compare these outcomes with empirical evidence. The inductive approach is generally based on searching for regularities and patterns in empirical data. Researches try to describe and explain them and new theories are derived as a result of such pursuits.

One of the most important research methods in natural sciences is the method of experiment. Researchers can construct artificial environments with required characteristics and conduct their experiments in optimum conditions. So far, the method of experiment is seldom available for scholars in social sciences. Economists (and other social scientists) have no labs in which they can verify their hypotheses, and conducting "experiments" means including even the whole population of a country without the possibility of repeating the test. There is no possibility of performing certain experiments that include unusual, unattainable, or extreme prerequisites on real populations at all, although such research could often be very valuable.

An important change occurred with the arrival of computers and the rise of computational methods in social sciences. The Monte Carlo method, developed in the 1940s in the Los Alamos National Laboratory,[1] was an important breakthrough due to the appearance of the simulation methods that were based on it. Discrete-event simulations allowed solving more advanced queuing problems than those soluble with an analytical approach. Continuous simulations (known as a System dynamics approach in social sciences) allowed studying complex systems and their behavior over time. Although these methods are very useful for certain tasks, they can hardly play the role of the laboratory in economics and other social sciences, because they work with a certain abstraction of the system. They do not strive to stand for the real system; (i.e. its components and their relationships). They rather mimic particular traits or properties of the system and investigate the impact of changes of the specific parameters on variables that correspond to the attributes of the system.

Since agent-based simulations emerged a couple of years ago, the possibilities moved further. They allow the simulation of individuals with their respective characteristics as

---

[1]Metropolis and Ulam 1949.

they interact with each other in order to pursue their own goals (i.e., the same behavior as the behavior of real people in real social system) and to watch the influence of the micro characteristics of the individuals on the macro-behavior of the system as a whole. Social science now has a tool that has the potential to be used as an experimental environment to test theories and extreme situations, to isolate particular phenomena of the complex behavior of a system and to serve as a support of other means of cognition of the reality.[2]

1.1   Statistical simulation

Simulation is the imitation of a particular process, thing or system in reality. Simulation mimics key characteristics and behaviors of the simulated entity (and often suppresses those less significant) in order to serve its purpose. It is typically cheaper, safer, easier, more attainable, or generally more efficient to perform the action in the simulation than to carry it out in reality. Simulations can help manage the complexity of the simulated system; they often allow one to repeatedly perform actions that are normally non-recurring and irreversible in practice, and to monitor those characteristics that are unavailable or difficult to access in reality. Various kinds of simulations are present in almost all fields of human activity. Thanks to the aforementioned characteristics, simulations are particularly suitable for testing, verifying, training, education, optimization, analysis, prediction, and similar purposes.

In statistics, simulation is a wide-spread method for solving probabilistic and dynamic tasks that are too complex for solving by analytical means. By analytical solution we mean a mathematical model that calculates an exact value from input parameters. For certain problems, an analytical solution is either too complicated or entirely unavailable. In such a case, we can use a simulation to perform the statistical experiment. The output of the experiment is not the exact value, but the estimation (point or interval) that is often sufficient for any practical use. Statistical simulation is closely connected with computing; because simulation experiments are typically computationally extensive tasks, and they are not soluble without enough computing capacity.[3]

Statistic simulation can be used as a valuable instrument for research in economics, finance, management, sociology and other social sciences. Over the years, with the development of technology and the boom of available computing capacity, various approaches to statistical simulation have emerged.

---

[2]Cahlík 2006, p. 15; Tesfatsion 2002.
[3]Dlouhý, Fábry, and Kuncová 2005, p. 9.

1.2 Main approaches to statistical simulation

1.2.1 Discrete event simulation

Discrete-event simulation has developed as a computer instrument to solve complex tasks in queuing theory (i.e., one the main branches of operational research) that were too intricate to solve in the classic analytical way. Discrete-event simulation simulates a system with certain inputs that pass through it. The inputs are processed inside according to the internal rules and finally leave the system. During this process, they can be delayed, grouped with other inputs, transformed, draw scarce resources, and so on. Simulation allows one to monitor the progress of, and measure, various characteristics like delays, time in the system, throughput, hoarding, utilization of resources, and many others.[4]

The name of the approach comes from the fact that the simulation does not treat time as continuous, but it builds a schedule of events that occur during the simulation (arrival of order, etc.). When the event happens, certain changes are triggered in the model, and there are no changes of model variables between such events. The simulator must indeed keep track of the simulation time in order to project its results into real-time measures.

Application of discrete-event simulation shifts from previous tasks of optimization of resources (i.e., an optimum number of cash desks in a shop to avoid queuing of customers, an optimum number of workers in a shift in order to fulfill orders, the optimum batch size to pack, etc.) in order to present models that support business process reengineering.

Discrete-event simulation is appropriate for the study of systems if their structure is well known. The analyst's task is to find the systems' optimum parameters or adjust their process according to the given objectives. Therefore, this form of simulation is sometimes called "process-centric simulation."

1.2.2 Continuous simulation and System dynamics

Continuous simulation is a method for the simulation of systems with complex internal interrelationships. The system contains entities with certain state variables that are dependent on each other, and their values change continuously (or we can at least treat the system as though they do). Dependencies of state variables are represented mainly by a set of differential equations, and the variables change continuously with respect to time because it is often simpler to express the relationships using derivatives of state variables than with the variables themselves. If the differential equations are simple enough, we

---

[4]Ibid., p. 33.

can solve the model analytically. However, when this is not possible, then it is the task of the simulation model to find a numerical solution.[5]

Continuous simulation was formerly used in natural science (physics, electrical engineering, meteorological models, etc.). Perhaps the most important application of continuous simulation in social science is System dynamics. This method is based on the assumption that in some cases the mere sum of parts does not render the system as a whole (i.e., there are certain properties in the system that do not belong to any of its fractions and so they emerge from the relationships among the system components). Therefore, it is appropriate to explore such systems using a holistic, rather than analytical, approach. The method was developed by Jay Forrester of the Massachusetts Technology Institute, Sloan School of Management. System dynamics models are based on a mental model of a system containing model elements (stocks and flows) that can be delayed and connected by feedback loops and other matters. The proponents of System dynamics emphasize the benefits of graphical representation of systems that lead to system thinking and consider it more important than the mere computation.[6] "Behind" the charts, there is a set of differential equations that embody the internal relationships among the state variables. By solving them, we can depict the state of the system at any moment of time.

The example of the System dynamics simulation could be a model of population in a country. There are a certain number of people in a particular moment of time; some are being born, some are dying, some immigrate, and some leave the country. Each of these factors changes the size of the population and has an impact on the number of people who are born and who die in that country.

System dynamics is appropriate for the research of systems if their behavior and internal relationships are known; however, it is not appropriate if their detailed internal structure is not known, too complex, or is not important for the respective purpose.

1.2.3   Agent-based simulations

The basic principle of agent-based simulations (or agent-based models) is the opposite of the principle of the aforementioned approaches. Unlike them, agent-based models are built from the bottom up (i.e., the analysts do not need to know the complex structure and operation of the system), but they start with the individual agents (as the constituents of the system), define their characteristics and behavior, and let them interact together in the agents' environment. The function of the system as a whole is not hard-coded to it intentionally by design, but it is rather a natural (and often even surprising) result of its agents' spontaneous conduct.[7]

Agent-based simulation appeared as one of many applications of multi-agent systems. Multi-agent systems belong to the big family of distributed information systems.

---

[5]Dlouhý, Fábry, and Kuncová 2005, p. 49.
[6]Forrester 1961; Forrester 1968.
[7]Tesfatsion 2002, p. 2.

Their theoretical principles have been elaborated upon for a relatively long time. We can see their origins in Neumann's and Ulam's cellular automata.[8] Since computing power requirements of agent-based models are relatively high, this method started to spread in the 90s with the massive dissemination of cheaper computers and pervasive growth of online networking.

Perhaps the most important part of the multi-agent system is the agents. The agents themselves are more or less "intelligent" chunks of computer code that are able to perceive and communicate with each other and react to stimuli in order to pursue their goals.[9] As an example, we can note the simulation of labor markets with certain agents-workers and agents-companies. Both workers and businesses are designed to maximize their utility (or profit, respectively). Workers can work for an employer and employers can hire workers. Both parties can communicate with each other, negotiate, and close deals. If the model is well balanced, phenomena like business cycles, fluctuating wage levels, unemployment, and other economical effects emerge in the system, even though no one had written them into the code.

Agent-based modeling is a suitable method for the study of problems where we know the characteristics of the atomic parts and are interested in the behavior of the entire system. These models are not often appropriate for undertaking classical optimization tasks because their numerical output does not need to correspond with real values. Nevertheless, they can be very useful (e.g., to see what influence the characteristics of the whole will have on the behavior of the individual elements, or to find out what unplanned properties and side effects emerge in the working system).

Unfortunately, despite a number of successful applications, this method does not seem to be widely implemented, and is not used outside of the scientific community. Most of this book is devoted to this approach.

1.2.4 Combined techniques (hybrid simulations)

Due to a fierce competition of simulation software on the market (among other reasons), its providers are constantly coming up with new functionalities, and tend to combine the individual techniques that were mentioned above. As a result of such pursuits, there are applications that contain more, or even all, of these approaches. For instance, GoldSim of GoldSim Technology Group is able to combine discrete-event and continuous simulation.[10] Anylogic of XJ Technologies can provide the functionality of all discrete-event, systems dynamic, and agent-based simulation.[11] Different methods are used either on the individual layers of simulation or within the single model; nonetheless, one of these methods often prevails in the respective software.

[8]Neumann 1966.
[9]Wooldridge 2002, p. 16.
[10]See http://www.goldsim.com/Content.asp?PageID=1 (visited on 24. 1. 2009)
[11]See http://www.xjtek.com/anylogic (visited on 24. 1. 2009)

The real benefit of the combination of methods is questionable due to deep differences among the mere principles of the aforementioned approaches. The combination of methods could be favorable for certain special purposes and applications; however, its potential is dubious, at least until somebody comes up with a smoother, more viable, approach towards synthesis than what is available today.

1.2.5 Serious gaming or participatory simulations

"Serious gaming" is a term that has been given to a wide group of computer games that are (besides entertainment) focused on certain "serious" purposes, like education, marketing, simulation, and so on. Serious gaming as a method of economic simulation is the newest,[12] potentially promising, computer-aided simulation approach. In principle, it is based on a similar foundation as agent-based simulations (i.e., a presence of a large number of agents that interact in a common environment). These micro-level interactions create complex and unpredictable macro-level characteristics of the system. Unlike agent-based simulations, where the agents are relatively simple "pieces of program code," in participatory simulation, agents are controlled by human players.[13]

The idea grew from the phenomenon of Massively Multiplayer Online Role-playing Games (MMORPG). MMORPG appeared in late 90s, and became very popular after the year 2000, when widely available, affordable, fast-Internet connections allowed a greater number of people to play games together on the Internet. MMORPG simulates a virtual world where players are represented by their virtual alter egos, called "avatars." They live in a simulated world, where they are able to gather assets, trade, communicate with the other players' avatars, make contracts, and so on. Today's MMORPGs are played by hundreds of thousands of people simultaneously, and so these virtual worlds could represent relatively large communities.

With the increasing popularity of MMORPGs, it was soon discovered that the same processes and phenomena appearing in their virtual economics (supply, demand, price mechanism, inflation, etc.) reflected those already present in the real world, even if they were not planned and incorporated into the software.[14] This was only one step away from the idea of using these virtual worlds for serious economic simulation. Providers of today's MMORPGs often take their virtual economics seriously, watch virtual macroeconomic indicators, or intervene in order to maintain the stability of the system. Some of them even publish macroeconomic reports for their online economy on a regular basis.[15]

---

[12]It is new in so far as the terminology including the name of the approach itself is still not settled at the time of writing this book.

[13]Guyot and Honiden 2006; Hackathorn 2007.

[14]Lehtiniemi 2008.

[15]E.g. see: http://ccp.vo.llnwd.net/o2/pdf/QEN_Q1-2008.pdf (Quarterly Economic Newsletter by EVE-Online)

On one hand, this is a very auspicious technology, because the intelligence of live players is indeed without comparison to any software agent, and so the complexity of the simulation and the precision of its results could be beyond any agent-based simulation. On the other hand, there are so many practical obstacles and difficulties with this method (including a certain amount of skepticism in the scientific community) that only time will tell if this method will succeed or not.

1.3 Chapter summary

Economics, as well as some other social sciences, lack a method of experiment. Testing of their theoretical concepts is challenging, and the only option, in many cases, of their application in reality. A possible solution could be a method of computer-aided, agent-based simulations that enables the simulation of economic entities and their interactions, and hence, the evaluation of hypotheses in a "safe" environment. The method emerged several years ago when it was allowed by increasing and more affordable computer performance, and can offer a substantial potential for the future.

Besides agent-based modeling, there are other methods available, like discrete-event simulation, system dynamics, various hybrid methods, and participatory simulations. Each of these can offer specific pros and cons and is suitable for a different kind of task.

Chapter 2

Multi-agent systems

Before we can discuss agent-based simulations as the main topic of this book, we cannot omit multi-agent systems as a distinct field of computer science. We can consider multi-agent systems as an alternative to the traditional computing paradigm that is based on von Neumann architecture. So-called von Neumann computer architecture is the most common design of present-day computer systems. It is described as a system containing a CPU and a shared memory for both program and data that accepts inputs and returns the results of its computations on the output. What is important, from our point of view, is that the classical monolithic computer is able to execute a single sequence of instructions, which operates on a single stream of data values.[1] It does not matter that current computer systems often contain several microprocessors (or at least more cores in the microprocessor) and use various techniques of multitasking, since their "intelligence" and behavior is always causal. In other words, they always do exactly what their designers and the developers of their software wanted them to do.

The main idea of multi-agent systems is different. It lacks a well defined structure and it is composed of multiple autonomous units called *agents*. There can be various forms of agents: robots, systems, pieces of computer program, and so on. For our purposes, if not stated otherwise, the agents are self-directed autonomous units of computer code. They are able to communicate with other agents and "feel" the percepts from the environment they reside in. The agents pursue their own goals on grounds of the information that they gain from the environment and from the other agents. They may or may not contain memory to store their data. Typically, none of the agents in the multi-agent system alone is able to encompass the whole task that the system has to solve. The solution does not come from the processing of a computer program with a hard-coded algorithm, but rather from the interaction of the individual agents. The intelligence of the system does not need to be intentional. The agents do not contain the program to solve the problem (or a part of the problem), but they are designed to *behave teleologically* (i.e., towards their own objectives). As each of the agents in the multi-agent system pursues its own goal, the aggregate operation of the system comes from their interaction and the entire system can produce a very complex, and perhaps not always foreseeable, behavior. Due to these characteristics, the multi-agent systems are a very appropriate

---

[1]Eigenmann and Lilja 1999.

pattern for such systems that are required to work in dynamic environments, systems that should be stable, durable, and scalable and that process loosely defined tasks.

2.1 Application domains

The aim of this chapter is not to give complete details of all application domains and areas of multi-agent systems, because, as multi-agent systems are a truly interdisciplinary domain, they overlap into various fields, like traffic engineering, power engineering, physics, statistics, economics, social science, geography, and many more. Instead, the author's intent is to map the principal areas of contemporary multi-agent research and the issues that are currently being solved.

Multi-agent approach is present and flourishing in many fields of contemporary computing. It is not easy to divide the multi-agent systems research into distinct categories, because most of them overlap and bear relations to each other. The following classification of multi-agent-related issues is one of many possible taxonomies. Multi-agent systems apply to:

- Robotics and cybernetics

- Artificial intelligence and machine learning

- Software engineering

- Networking

- Search engines and text mining

- Electronic commerce and trade

- Simulation and modeling

- and other fields...

2.1.1 Robotics and cybernetics

Agent research in robotics is tremendously extensive. There are hundreds to thousands of articles in this subfield published annually. Among research topics, there are multi-agent robotic navigation,[2] multi-agent control and self-reconfigurable robots,[3] robotic cooperation and coordination (robotic soccer games, as one of the instruments of such

---

[2]Munoz-Salinas et al. 2005; Ambastha et al. 2005.
[3]Casal 2000.

research, are noticed from time to time, even in popular media),[4] multi-agent robotic vision,[5] and many others.

NASA's Deep Space I probe (launched in 1998) was driven by the Remote Agent distributed control system based on multi-agent principles; it was fault-tolerant and able to make quick decisions without the necessity of human intervention, which would be impractical.[6]

2.1.2   Artificial intelligence and machine learning

Multi-agent systems belong to a wide family of artificial intelligence and are tightly interconnected with its other fields, like neural networks, genetic algorithms, fuzzy logic, and others. The following topics are (among others) under research in this subfield: distributed artificial intelligence,[7] multi-agent reinforcement learning,[8] and automated decision making.[9]

2.1.3   Software engineering

Approaches to developing agents as the basic units of multi-agent systems brought new issues to the theory of programming and programming languages. Although still the most common in the development of multi-agent systems, object-oriented languages are not wholly suitable for such purposes, due to deep differences between objects and agents. Unlike objects, agents are autonomous, active, self-managed software entities; and if the object-oriented language is used, these properties must be transformed into the instruments of the object-oriented approach. Therefore, there are many efforts to develop an agent-oriented programming language with the result of languages like Agent0,[10] GOAL,[11] AgentSpeak,[12] 3APL,[13] and others. Agent-oriented programming is mentioned, from time to time, as a new programming paradigm (especially in the field of distributed information systems) that should emerge from object-oriented programming and promote it to a new level – the same way as object- oriented programming developed from the structured programming.[14] Up to now, most of the applications did not go beyond research, experimental, or educational purposes. There will be more on agent-oriented programming languages in chapter 5.

---

[4]Shukri and Shaukhi 2008.
[5]Wnuk, Fulkerson, and Sudol 2006.
[6]Pell et al. 1998.
[7]Weiss 1999.
[8]Kok and Vlassis 2006.
[9]Kakas and Moraitis 2003.
[10]Shoham 1991.
[11]See http://mmi.tudelft.nl/~koen/goal.php (visited on 6. 4. 2009)
[12]Rao 1996.
[13]See http://www.cs.uu.nl/3apl (visited on 6. 4. 2009)
[14]Vecchiola et al. 2003.

Besides agent-oriented programming, a lot of work was done in the area of agent-oriented design, agent frameworks, and agent-oriented methodologies. They will be discussed more in depth in chapters B and 6.

Recently, a lot of study has been devoted to the synthesis of multi-agent systems, web services,[15] and service-oriented architecture.[16]

2.1.4   Networking

The Internet alone has many characteristics of multi-agent systems: it is composed of autonomous units that communicate mutually, each of them has its own objectives and wishes, and there are common communication standards; aside from these, there is no "central plan" within its structure. Therefore, the Internet is very stable with a minimum number of vulnerable points, and theoretically, it can grow almost indefinitely.

Present multi-agent related research in Internet technologies deals mainly with Internet routing. As the current OSPF routing algorithm poses a certain amount of limitation, the agent technologies have a chance to outperform it and replace it in the future.[17] Another subject of research is routing in ad-hoc mobile networks,[18] sensor networks,[19] and security.[20]

2.1.5   Search engines and text analysis

Searching has always been a crucial Internet service; however, after the rise of Google it became a true industry. Although search engines before Google were often based on large supercomputers, Google used the concept of widespread, distributed architecture heavily.[21] Since the number of Web pages published on the Internet is skyrocketing every year, it imposes huge demands on computational power and bandwidth consumed by the search engine, and so any centralized solution is no longer feasible. Multi-agent systems seem to be a fructuous concept in this field. In recent years, there was a lot of work done in multi-agent Web searching,[22] data mining,[23] meta-search,[24] and other relevant topics.

---

[15]Shafiq, Ding, and Fensel 2006; Zhu and Shan 2005.

[16]Luo et al. 2007.

[17]Caro and Dorigo 1998.

[18]Macker et al. 2005; Peysakhov et al. 2006; Kheirabadi and Mohammadi 2007; Manvi and Kakkasageri 2008.

[19]Martínez et al. 2007.

[20]Ping et al. 2008.

[21]Brin and Page 1998.

[22]Gopalan and Akilandeswari 2005.

[23]Niimi and Konishi 2004.

[24]Keyhanipour et al. 2005.

2.1.6 Electronic commerce and trade

The adoption of technologies allowing virtualization of real-world objects and their integration into existing business models drive the automation of business processes and interaction in electronic marketplaces. Multi-agent systems can offer distributed, robust, and dynamic environments of autonomous software entities containing business logic on behalf of users and organizations. The open issues for multi-agent systems in electronic markets include ontologies, semantic models, trading models, trust and reputation management, and others.

Recent works in this area are concerned with dynamic automated supply chain formation,[25] agents and electronic marketplaces,[26] agents for electronic auctions and automated negotiation,[27] and so on.

2.1.7 Simulation and modeling

Simulation and modeling based on the multi-agent systems (agent-based modeling) is perhaps the most important and heavily researched subfield of multi-agent systems. Due to their characteristics, mentioned above, multi-agent systems provide a unique simulation platform for many tasks. Some of them are mentioned in the following text.

EpisSimS was the simulation of spatial aspects of the spread of pandemic influenza[28] that was simulated on an artificial population of almost 19 million people. It was constructed to match the demographics of southern California (one of the largest population models used in the agent-based simulation).

Agent-based simulations are popular in traffic engineering because their models can mimic traffic very accurately and they can include the behavioral patterns of travelers. Although they are still relatively simple to develop, the results are synoptic and well comparable with reality. Hence, traffic management models are developed for all air traffic,[29] road transportation,[30] and even pedestrian behavior.[31] They can be used as a tool for capacity planning, unveiling high-load points with a risk of forming congestions, road construction, and so on.

Power engineering is another field where agent-based simulations can be used. For instance, the model simulating electricity balancing in networks was developed in order to find ways to reduce imbalances caused by wind electricity production.[32]

---

[25]Chaibdraa and Müller 2006; Tian and Tianfield 2007.
[26]Dogac et al. 1998.
[27]Garcia, Lopes, and Bentes 2001.
[28]Stroud et al. 2007.
[29]Tumer and Agogino 2007; Pechoucek and Sislak 2009.
[30]Dresner and Stone 2006.
[31]Klügl and Rindsfüser 2007.
[32]Kok et al. 2008.

Agent-based simulations are a good technology for solving various security-related simulation tasks, including designing and analyzing security systems, protocols, and policies that aim to protect fixed-site facilities against intrusions by external threats, as well as unauthorized acts by insiders[33] and the analyses of terrorist attacks, like the BioWar model. It simulates individuals during bioterrorist attacks as agents who are embedded in social, health, and professional networks. It tracks the incidence of background and maliciously-introduced diseases, healthcare-seeking behaviors, absenteeism patterns, and pharmaceutical purchases, information that is useful for syndromic and behavioral surveillance algorithms.[34]

Progressive technologies were always used for military purposes, and so it is no wonder that agent-based simulations are developed by army experts to support their tasks. Cioppa et al. present the examples of military analyses performed by this method. Exploring the ability of the U.S. Army's network-based Future Force to perform with degraded communications, or studies of how unmanned surface vehicles can be used in force protection missions,[35] belong to the problems being solved.

Probably the biggest group of agent-based simulations is that which deals with economic and financial issues and topics from other social sciences, particularly sociology and psychology.

LeBaron[36] focuses on agent-based models of financial markets and investor conduct. The models can be used for the research of behavior of the markets and prediction of their future moves. Agent-based models are also a tool for testing the impact and effects of public policies and for finding their optimum levels and fine tuning.[37] Examples include the assessment of the efficiency of investment incentives,[38] a model of optimization of tax-benefit systems for the reduction of poverty,[39] and many others. The method can also be used for testing and evaluating concepts and theories in economics (e.g., in game theory-related research[40]). Another kind of models deals with the optimization of supply chains,[41] personnel scheduling management,[42] and other managerial topics. In sociological research, there are numerous examples of agent-based models published, like the simulation of gender stratification,[43] research on whether increasing punish-

---

[33]Ustun, Yilmaz, and Smith 2006.
[34]Carley et al. 2006.
[35]Cioppa, Lucas, and Sanchez 2004.
[36]LeBaron and Winker 2008; LeBaron 2006.
[37]Lempert 2002; Brenner and Werker 2009.
[38]Šalamon 2008a.
[39]Sallila 2010.
[40]Ohdaira and Terano 2009.
[41]Wadhwa and Bibhushan 2006.
[42]Sabar, Montreuil, and Frayret 2009.
[43]Robison-Cox, Martell, and Emrich 2007.

ments has an effect on reducing crime,[44] the model of marriage formation and marital distribution,[45] models of racial segregation,[46] and many others.

Most of this book will be devoted to agent-based models in economics and other social sciences.

2.2   Chapter summary

Multi-agent systems are a special kind of information system based on the inter-action of multiple, independent, autonomous, goal-oriented units called agents. From their behavior and relationships, certain properties develop that have unique characteristics.

There are a handful of domains where multi-agent systems are implemented, including robotics and cybernetics, artificial intelligence and machine learning, software engineering, networking, search engines and text mining, electronic commerce and trade, simulation and modeling.

---

[44]Rauhut and Junker 2009.
[45]Mumcu and Saglam 2008.
[46]Chen et al. 2005.

Chapter 3
Agents

3.1 Agent environments

Before we start studying agents, we must first discuss the environments where the agents operate, because, as we will see later, they represent crucial limiting factors of the multi-agent systems and their properties directly influence the architecture and behavior of the agents.

Agent environments can be categorized along various traits, but the most cited is probably the classification presented by Russell and Norvig.[1] They organize the environments according to the following properties:

- *Accessible* vs. *inaccessible* – if it is possible to gather full and complete information about the environment in the moment, then the environment is accessible. Typically, only virtual environments can be accessible, because in reality, all sensors provide an input that is biased and incomplete up to some extent. There are so many potential percepts in the real world that it would be impossible to record and process them in real time (even if agent's sensors were infinitely sensitive). In fully accessible environments, the agents do not need to create models of the world in their memories, because it can get any needed information from the environment at any time.

- *Deterministic* vs. *non-deterministic* – if an action performed in the environment causes a definite effect, the environment is deterministic. Definite effect means that any action of the agent leads to the intended and expected results and there is no room for uncertainty. Of course, if the environment is inaccessible for the agent, it will be probably non-deterministic, at least from its point of view. Turn-based games are an example of a typical deterministic environment, whereas a room with a thermostat (where the thermostat is the agent) is an example of non-deterministic environment, because the action of the thermostat does not necessarily lead to the change of temperature (if, for instance, a window is open).

- *Static* vs. *dynamic* – the environment is static when the agent is the only entity that changes the environment in the moment. If it changes during the agent's action

---

[1]Russell and Norvig 1995, p. 46.

(i.e., the state of the environment is contingent on time), it is dynamic. Again, often real environments are dynamic (e.g., traffic in a city) and just some artificial environments are static (consider turn-based games like chess again).

- *Discrete* vs. *continuous* – this depends on whether a number of possible actions in the environment are finite or infinite. If the agent just has a certain set of possible actions that it can do in the moment, then the environment is discrete. Otherwise, when the agent has theoretically an infinite number of options, the environment is continuous. Suppose that roulette is a discrete environment. The agent can place a wager on a certain, limited number of betting areas. On the other hand, the legal system is a continuous environment. People have theoretically an unlimited number of options how to, for example, close deals or defend themselves before a court.

- *Episodic* vs. *non-episodic* – episodic environment is the environment where the agent operates in certain segments (episodes) that are independent of each other. The agent's state in one episode has no impact on its state in another one. Human life exists in a non-episodic environment,[2] because all of our past experiences influence our conduct in the future. An operating system, on the other hand, is an episodic environment, as we can reinstall it. Then programs-agents can be installed on a "clean system" with no conjunction with the same programs installed on the old system.

The author of this book adds another characteristic that is especially important in agent-bases simulations. We can distinguish the environments also according to their spatial characteristics:

- *Dimensional* vs. *dimensionless* – if spatial characteristics are important factors of the environment and the agent considers space in its decision making, then the environment is dimensional. If the agents do not take space into account, then the environment is dimensionless. Real environments are typically dimensional, as we naturally feel and count with spatial characteristics of our surroundings. In the virtual environments, such characteristics are not always important. For example, as stock markets are almost fully electronic today, it does not matter where somebody is present physically, since he or she can buy or sell shares on theoretically any market in the world. In such an environment, spatial characteristics have no influence on the agents' decision making, and therefore it is dimensionless.

As we will see later, the design of the agents depends heavily on the type of environment they reside in. Of course, the more inaccessible, non-deterministic, non-episodic, dynamic and continuous the environment, the more difficult is developing the agent.

---

[2]...unless we are Hindu.

As we can see from the aforementioned list, the environment is a kind of *abstraction*. Specific categorization of an environment mostly depends on how the agent perceives it. Several times, we have used chess as an example of an "easy" environment; however, consider a robot that should be able to play chess with a human on a common wooden chessboard. Normally, if we think of chess as an abstract world with certain rules, we need not think of where to place a piece. We simply decide to move it to a certain square described by its coordinates on the chessboard and that's it. In reality, the robot could place a piece a little bit left or right within the square, and so there is theoretically an infinite number of options how to do it. It means that the environment must be comprehended as an abstract concept and the agent's point of view is crucial. This is, however, the way people think. We tend to simplify reality into an abstract concept in order to filter out insignificant factors and focus on those that are important.

3.2 Agent characteristics

In previous chapters, we came to the description of the multi-agent system as a system composed of autonomous agents. Now we should discuss more deeply what the agents are, what kinds of them we know, and what characteristics they have.

As there are many definitions of multi-agent systems, there are many definitions of agents as well. For instance, Wooldridge and Jennings state:

> "An agent is a computer system that is situated in some environment, and that is capable of autonomous action in this environment in order to meet its design objectives."[3],[4]

This definition is limited to artificial agents. In a more general way, we can even consider agents as people, groups, or organizations. From this point of view, a better and more general definition could be given as follows:

> "Agents are autonomous decision-making units with diverse characteristics."[5]

According to this definition, an agent could be almost anything or anyone that is able to make self-directed decisions. For practical reasons, it is useful to distinguish agents as several key groups according to their physical substance.

- *Physical (or real) agents* – the tangible, artificial entities that exist in the real world, such as robots, intelligent sensors, probes, and similar automatic devices

---

[3]It is necessary to understand "computer system" in a very broad meaning (including robots, intelligent sensors, etc.)
[4]Wooldridge and Jennings 1995.
[5]Macal and North 2006.

- *Software agents* – chunks of software code that are capable of autonomous action; it is possible to conceive of them as objects, software components, or other pieces of program code (computer viruses can be considered to be software agents of a certain kind)

- *Natural agents* – animals and humans. The behavior of artificial agents (both physical and software) is often inspired and compared to the attributes of living beings.[6]

For our purposes, the exact definition is not crucial, and instead of getting stuck in philosophical nuances, it will be perhaps more helpful to discuss the typical characteristics of agents in order to become familiar with agents and multi-agent systems.

Agents are equipped to *communicate* with other agents and *perceive* their environment. Some sources do not distinguish between agents' communication and perception, but according to the author, these two modes of interaction should be treated separately, because unlike humans, the ability of communication and perception is distinct in the agent world.[7] Communication is considered to be the intentional sending and receiving of information to and from other agents, whereas perception is just the sensation of the unstructured information from the agent's environment (see figure 3.1). *Reactiveness* or the ability to perceive the environment and to react to the percepts from there, is one of the basic agent characteristics.

There can be agents without perception functions (which is rather common in software agents of agent-based simulations), whereas agents without communication abilities are scarcer, as communication is what differentiates a system from just a bunch of individual agents. Nonetheless, as we will see further, there are examples of agents that need not communicate directly with each other to constitute a multi-agent system.

Communication is a necessary prerequisite to their agent's more advanced interactive abilities like cooperation, coordination, and competition. We will call them *social abilities*. Agents do not pursue their goals alone, but often in the relationships with other agents. The most important characteristics of multi-agent systems do not come from the agents' internal intelligence, but they emerge from these abilities. Agents can ask other agents for help while solving their tasks, because agents can have different skills and some tasks can be soluble only when more types of agents cooperate. On the other hand, sometimes agents can pursue conflicting objectives, and consequently not all can be indulged, and then competition among them can take place.

Communication and perception is only one side of agent abilities. On the other side, there is agent *action* (i.e., the capability of acting autonomously on the basis of the agent's reasoning, no matter how pursued). *Autonomy* means that the performance or non-

---

[6]The reader can also find another terms for the same categories: robotic agents, computational agents and biological agents (Franklin and Graesser 1997)

[7]People cannot communicate without sensing their surroundings (hearing, seeing, etc.), whilst agents can.

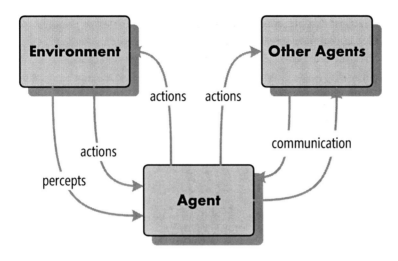

Figure 3.1 – Agent interaction model – agents interact with each other and with their environment. They communicate with other agents, draw percepts from the environment, influence and can be influenced by actions of the environment and other agents.

performance of action depends solely on an agent's decision. There are various modes of agent decision making (see below), from very simple ones to those more sophisticated, but the action is always a result of the agent's assessment. It represents one of the most substantial differences between agents and objects, where objects have no choice of what to do – if their method is called, they simply have to perform their code (and do not philosophize about it). Agents are autonomous, which means that they could be asked for the action, but it is up to them whether they will act or not.[8]

Figure 3.1 illustrates how the agent can act either towards the environment or towards other agents. There can be a handful of examples of interaction with the environment. Real agents – like robots – could, for example, move, carry things, and so on. Software agents could, for example, draw a line in their environment or do similar actions. The action towards the other agents is relatively straightforward, in the case of physical agents (e.g., one robot could give something to another one, or try to destroy it, etc.). In the case of software agents, the actions performed on other agents are, technically, mostly mediated by the environment.

If agents have to operate autonomously, they need a certain foundation to ground their decisions on. Agents have goals that they strive to accomplish and the goals play the role of such a foundation. The agents act in order to fulfill them. All actions and decisions are evaluated with respect to the agent's objectives and the agent performs

---

[8]Wooldridge 2002, p. 25.

only those actions that are in accordance with its goals. The other possible actions are omitted. Hence, *goal orientation* is another fundamental agent characteristic. Goals can be expressed in various ways. They can be represented either symbolically as a desired state of the agent world, or they can be embodied indirectly in the agent's preset behaviors and their interaction with the environment.

Initiative is another agent characteristic that stems from their goal orientation and autonomy. Agents are able to act not only when they are explicitly asked for, but also on their own when they assume that it is necessary to fulfill the goal. Such spontaneous action is indeed dependent on external conditions and can be triggered by various events, but unlike the case of objects, it is not needed to "call" the agent in order to perform a reaction on such event. Again, there are several ways that an agent can behave initiatively. The initiative does not require the agent to be equipped with symbolic artificial intelligence.

This would be a good place to introduce an example. Consider an Internet router.[9] Simply said, the basic function of a router is to receive data packets through its input port and to decide what outbound interface they should be passed to.[10] Consider a router with two outbound ports. When it receives a packet of data on its input, it evaluates it according to a certain set of rules applied to the destination address of the packet and decides to either forward it to the first or to the second output interface, or to drop it eventually. Although each router in the Internet principally does not "know" anything more than which connected wires it should forward incoming packets to, the complex of millions of routers constitutes the system that is able to send data from one place to any other location in the world. Hence, from a certain point of view, we can see that the Internet could be considered to be a kind of multi-agent system with the routers serving as the agents. It represents a good demonstration of the unique ability of multi-agent systems to build complex global behavior from a relatively simple functionality on the unit-level.

Furthermore, a simple router could be understood as an example of an agent that lacks the communication function, because it can just perceive the environment (incoming packages) and act (forwarding packages) without any additional direct communication and coordination with other routers. In fact, as was already mentioned, a modern-day router is a much more complicated apparatus which often does possess communication functionality and is able to actively coordinate its function with the other routers (using protocols like OSPF, RIP, BGP, etc.). Thus, we can also witness other agent characteristics like goal-orientation, social abilities or initiative.

To sum up, the agent characteristics that we have described above are:

---

[9]I will avoid using thermostat as the example of an agent that is very popular (and thus, perhaps clichéd) illustration in multi-agent related textbooks.

[10]We can pass over the fact that contemporary routers are profoundly sophisticated devices with much more complicated function.

- *Social abilities* – communication, coordination, cooperation, competition, and so on

- *Initiative* – the ability to act proactively, not just perform what they are asked to do

- *Goal-orientation* – pursuing own objectives and behaving in order to reach them,

- *Autonomy* of decision making and action,

- *Reactiveness* – the ability to react to percept or information from outside.

This specification is one of many possible. Almost each author writing about agent technologies introduces his or her own definition of agent properties. Although there are various rosters, they usually do not differ much in fact and no matter how many items the list contains, it often bears more or less the same gist.

Despite differences in definitions and terminology among authors dealing with agent technologies, there is a good consensus on the basic principles and characteristics of agents. The same cannot be said about the approaches to their implementation. As agent technologies evolved in different application domains for various purposes, more concepts were developed. For purposes of this book, two main paradigms are relevant: *reactive agents* and *deliberative agents*.

The main difference between them lies in their reasoning. Deliberative agents use means of symbolic artificial intelligence. They build more or less complex models of the outer world in their memory and their decisions stem from it. Numerous kinds of technologies can be used for retaining such model: various data structures, logical formulae, neural networks, and others. The agent receives percepts and information from outside, includes it into the model in its memory, and makes a decision that should be optimal on the basis of known information. The decision then leads to the action.

Reactive agents contain no symbolic artificial intelligence and they create no models of world. Their intelligence is not the inherent trait of agents, but it comes directly from their interaction with each other and the environment instead. The main characteristic of a reactive agent is its

> orthogonal decomposition: there are no central, functional modules, such as a perception module, a reasoning module, a learning module, a central representation, and so on. Instead, the agent consists of a completely distributed, decentralized set of competence modules (also called behaviors). These modules do all the perception, "reasoning," learning and representation necessary for achieving a particular competence.[11]

Both approaches have pros and cons that will be discussed in the following chapters.

---

[11]Maes 1991.

Beside the foregoing ones, there are many other agent taxonomies. Russel and Norvig classify them according to their complexity to four groups (simple reflex agents, reflex agents with state, goal based agents and utility based agents).[12] Agents can be classified by their mobility as static and mobile,[13] and there are many other categorizations, groups and subgroups in the literature.

---

[12]Russell and Norvig 1995, pp. 40-45.
[13]Nwana 1996.

3.3 Reactive agents

Reactive agents (it is possible to meet *behavior-based agents* or *purely reactive agents* different names of similar phenomena[14]) are one of two most important paradigms of agency. Their appellation comes from the fact that they do not reason about their environment by means of artificial intelligence; they do not create models of their environment in order to plan further actions, but simply react to percepts and information from there. Reactive agents are a simple, though extremely important, type of agents. Thanks to their relative simplicity, they are easier (and less expensive) to develop and debug; they are (at least, theoretically) more reliable and have lower demands on the computational power. Due to these characteristics, they are suitable for applications of agent-based models, where a large number of relatively simple agents is typically required, either in their pure, fundamental manner, or as a part of hybrid agents (see section 3.5). Regardless of their simplicity, reactive agents can constitute very complex and large systems.

The idea of reactive agents was promoted by Rodney Brooks for robotics and later generalized for artificial intelligence. Brooks pointed out that the traditional artificial intelligence approaches are based on a top-down principle.

> Artificial intelligence started as a field whose goal was to replicate human level intelligence in a machine.[15]

The goal was to understand and describe how human intelligence "works" and to mimic it. However, our intelligence did not appear suddenly one day, it developed gradually from simpler forms over thousands of years. Consequently, artificial intelligence should, according to Brooks, go this way as well. The intelligent behavior should not be embedded in an intelligent entity that creates models of world in its memory and performs reasoning over them, but it should emerge from the complex interactions of many simple units.

Brooks also introduces terms such as *situatedness*, *embodiment*, *intelligence* and *emergence*[16] that are widely used in reactive-agents theory. As a robotics scientist, he defines these terms for robots, but they can be conveniently used for the agents as well.

Situatedness – The agents are situated in the world (i.e., they do not deal with abstract descriptions, but directly interact with the real system). As an example, consider an automatic vacuum cleaner that trundles over a house and sucks up dust. Situatedness means that it has no map of the house in its memory (e.g., to orientate, avoid obstacles,

---

[14]Some authors treat purely reactive and behavior-based agents as two separate groups (Jung, Cheng, and Zelinsky 1998); others deem it as the same principle (Maes 1991). For the purpose of this book, distinction of these categories is not needed and we will consider reactive agents, purely reactive agents, and behavior-based agents as synonyms.

[15]Brooks 1991b.

[16]Brooks 1991a.

etc.), but it possess a camera or other sensors and reacts on the immediate percepts it receives from these.

Embodiment – The agents are physically present in the world – they directly influence the dynamics of the world and get instant, natural feedback on their sensors. Consider unmanned aircraft as the autonomous reactive agent. If the aircraft decreases the thrust of its engine, it will detect the descending altitude on its altimeter in a moment as a physical answer to a lower uplift on its wing caused by a lower throttle.

Embodiment could be a problem in the case of software agents as they do not exist in real world, but in a simulated reality instead. The virtual world must contain a set of rules that are universally valid within it, just as physical laws are universally valid in the real world. This could be sometimes tricky to accomplish.

Intelligence – agents behave intelligently, but the source of the intelligence is not just an intentional algorithm. It comes not only from within the agents, but also from their physical interaction with the world.

In the late 90s, Sony developed a robotic dog called Aibo that was marketed as a toy.[17] Aibo was able to find a charger when low on power and recharge automatically. Because it would be an extremely complex task to simply find a normal power plug and recharge directly, it was delivered with a special recharging station with an easily tracked checker pattern, so the robot was able to identify it and connect itself to the charger. A part of its intelligence was not entrenched in the machine, but came from the characteristics of the environment where the robot operated.

Emergence – the intelligence of the system as a whole comes from the system's interactions with the world and from interactions between its components. It is hard to discover the specific part of the system that caused certain macro-level action.[18]

A good example of emergence is the Internet as was discussed above. It is perhaps impossible to say that any particular router, wire, or any other component caused a successful delivery of data packets. Instead, there are common rules (embodied in the TCP/IP protocol family) that all routers have to obey because packets are delivered from point A to point B.

The aforementioned characteristics of reactive agents are good for the understanding of their principles, but are, however, not entirely practical for application because Brook's work is tightly connected with robots and physical agents (interaction with the physical world is even considered the crucial component). In the case of software agents and agent-based modeling, some assumptions are not realistic or practical (one of the problems was mentioned above in the definition of embodiment).

---

[17]The production was stopped in 2006. Sony ceased to develop it because sales did not reach their expectations. Aibo probably appeared before its time. See http://www.sony.net/SonyInfo/ IR/info/presen/05q3/qfhh7c000008adfe.html (visited on 16.5.2009)

[18]It is also a reason, why debugging of multi-agent systems is not easy.

Reactive agents have a specific architecture. The agent consists of decentralized competence modules that are often called behaviors. Behaviors are organized by various means, depending on the particular architecture, into a global structure that constitutes the whole agent. There is typically no separation of functional modules like sensors, planning or decision-making units, but the sensory input is directly connected to a particular behavior and output is generated directly by the module as well.

Brooks offered so-called *subsumption architecture* for reactive mobile robots;[19] this is one of the most influential architectures used in reactive agents. Its idea is based on the principle of several layers, where each layer contains a simple behavior (action) that is triggered by certain conditions. The structure of each layer corresponds to the following pattern:

$$\textbf{if } \text{condition } \textbf{then } \text{do this} \tag{3.1}$$

The lower the layer, the higher its priority is. On the bottom-most layers are the actions with the highest priority that agent must perform before other kinds of actions, like security-related tasks. For example:

$$\textbf{if } \text{there is an obstacle ahead } \textbf{then } \text{change direction} \tag{3.2}$$

The higher the level, the less common and more specific the behavior is. The subsumption architecture is a relatively simple approach on how to deal with the input from more sensors (eventually conflicting), more goals (eventually conflicting as well), while keeping the system simple and robust.

In order to demonstrate the characteristics of reactive agents, it could be helpful to introduce an example. Recent military conflicts in Iraq and Afghanistan brought new trends of using unmanned vehicles and aircrafts and autonomous robots for special tasks. The U.S. armed forces deployed 4,000 robots during the war in Iraq and Afghanistan[20] and it is probable that their usage will grow as they can save the lives of soldiers and the money of taxpayers. The following example was inspired by this effort.

A defense manufacturer got an order to develop an automatic airborne system that should be able to eliminate terrorist groups in uneasily accessible terrain at night. Prerequisites stipulated that the units of the system (unmanned aircraft) cannot communicate on radio, to avoid being detected and/or jammed, and they should be able to observe a relatively large area (up to tens of miles). Because the army assumes deploying the system in zones where nobody but terrorists should be, then if the system detects a group of enemies on its infrared cameras, it should assault them immediately. The attack should be as precisely targeted as possible in order to save ammunition and not make needless damages. Engineers calculated the limits of weight of explosives carried

---

[19]Brooks 1990.
[20]Minkel 2008.

by the unmanned aircrafts, so that no single unit can bear enough ammo to destroy the whole target of average size (more units must be involved).

Each unit is a small automatic, unpiloted airplane equipped with several cameras working in the infrared spectrum to detect people at night, a GPS system to identify its vertical and horizontal position, explosives to exterminate the target, and a steering computer built on the basis of subsumption architecture. The architecture consists of six layers:

Layer	Behavior
6	**if** true **then** fly straight
5	**if** a spot underneath **then** hit the target
4	**if** thermal spot seen **then** head there
3	**if** over 1500 feet AGL[21] **then** descend
2	**if** outside perimeter **then** turn right
1	**if** under 1000 feet AGL **then** climb

Figure 3.2 – Scheme of subsumption architecture of the multi-agent system of unmanned combat aircrafts. The lowest layers have the highest priority and therefore solve the most urgent (typically safety-related) tasks. The higher we go, the less critical and more common tasks occur.

The sensors, like infrared cameras, altimeter, GPS, and so on are connected directly to the respective layers and provide relatively high level input like "our altitude is 800 feet" or "we are outside the operation perimeter," or "we see a thermal spot" (the thermal spot is defined by a region of certain threshold size and temperature).

The system works as follows: before the action, the operation perimeter is set into the internal GPSs of the units. It is done for the circumscription of the operational area in order to not jeopardize civilians and allies. Then the units (let's say tens of them) are deployed inside the area (note that given the layer 2, the eventual deployment outside the perimeter would necessarily cause the whole system to fail, because all the airplanes would whirl on the spot until they run out of fuel).

The lowest-level behavior assures that if the aircraft was too low, it should ascend a little bit (it could get lower even unintentionally, due to rising terrain, wind or negative thermal lift). Note that it is not a coincidence that this behavior is two levels under the behavior of descending in the case of the altitude being too high. It is indeed much more dangerous to be too low than too high; the behavior of ascending must have a higher priority and hence, be on the lower layer.

On the second layer, there is a behavior that assures the aircraft will stay in the operational perimeter (if the unit crosses its borders, it turns until it is back where it is sup-

---

[21] Above Ground Level

posed to be). This behavior makes the aircraft appear to fly in a zigzag pattern within the operational area.

If a thermal spot is observed (which should represent a group of enemies), the unit changes its direction to this location. If the spot grows as the aircraft gets closer, the direction of the aircraft is naturally reinforced. If the spot disappears (e.g., because it was just an animal or another false alarm), the plane would simply fly straight until another behavior is triggered.

If one of the units explodes, others will see the detonation as a thermal blotch and turn in that direction. If any targets still remain in the area, other aircrafts will get there "lured" by their thermal spots and probably hit them. Otherwise, they will continue in random flight.

The point is that a relatively simple system without any kind of artificial intelligence, which is in fact driven by six conditions while its units are prevented from mutual communication, is able to behave intelligently and pursue relatively demanding objectives, search targets, and effectively cooperate on their extermination (if one aircraft finds an enemy, others are automatically vectored there).

There are indeed many practical drawbacks: how to distinguish between enemies and allies or civilians, how to distinguish between a group of people and, say, a herd of animals, how to avoid collisions of airborne units, how to avoid puzzling units by the heat of dead bodies and soil (warmed by the blast) and bombing the same place over and over, the question of the sensitivity of infrared cameras, and many more; but, they are not important for our example.[22]

However, why not expand our example in order to demonstrate further properties of subsumption architecture and reactive agents? What should be, for instance, done if the aircraft is low on fuel? Let's say it is not a good idea to let it simply fall anywhere. There are two possibilities – it could either self-destruct or return to the base for a safe landing. The first case is the simpler one. It would require including one more behavior between the layers 4 and 5:

$$\textbf{if } \text{low on fuel } \textbf{then } \text{detonate} \qquad (3.3)$$

This case is very simple, because after performing this behavior, the unit is destroyed and so the program is terminated.

If we want the aircraft to fly to the base and land safely, the problem is much more complicated. In the classical subsumption architecture described above, the solution would make the program less limpid. It would be necessary to adjust layers 2, 4, 5, and 6 and implement the condition of "not being low on fuel" in order to perform the

---

[22]Of course, the aforementioned example was contemplated solely as a demonstration of the concept of multi-agent system based on reactive agents using subsumption architecture. A real deployment of a similar system in a combat operation would indeed require much deeper technical analysis and the consideration of countless additional technical, tactical, security and ethical issues.

respective behaviors. Besides that, we would need to add another layer with the behavior "fly home." The architecture can then look, for instance, like Figure 3.3.

Layer	Behavior
7	if true then fly straight
6	if low on fuel then head to home
5	if inside perimeter and a spot underneath then hit the target
4	if thermal spot seen and not low on fuel then head there
3	if over 1500 feet AGL then descend
2	if outside perimeter and not low on fuel then turn right
1	if under 1000 feet AGL then climb

Figure 3.3 – Scheme of subsumption architecture of multi-agent system of unmanned combat aircrafts with the added ability of returning to the base.

One can ask why we simply do not implement a variable containing the information that the unit is in "returning mode." But remember that this approach is based solely on reaction to the environment; the reactive agents in their pure version have no internal symbolic representation of knowledge, and the perception of the surrounding world is its representation alone. Besides that, the individual behaviors in subsumption architecture do not share a common memory. They are connected to input sensors and output effectors directly. Therefore, it is correct to test the quantity of fuel for every operation cycle.

It is apparent that such a solution is impractical. Just a slight adjustment requires substantial changes in code and the outcome is much more complex than the original version.[23] For any additional function, the code would become much more complex with rising risk of errors, side-effects, and unintended behaviors.

Due to these drawbacks, many modifications and competitive approaches of subsumption architecture have appeared. *Dynamic subsumption architecture*[24] is one of them. It is more flexible because it allows for the dynamic reconfiguration of its behaviors during the operation. The system is set to a certain mode dependent on a current situation and the architecture of the agent changes accordingly. Therefore, the same agent can react to the same percepts differently, along with its mode. The behaviors are not only organized in vertical layers, but also in horizontal columns. Each column represents a subagent – a functional module, like a sensor, solver, and so on (though the individual behaviors are still connected directly to their input and effector devices). The individual behaviors are then contained in cells. If certain conditions trigger a change of mode,

---

[23]Nevertheless the code is still simplified, because it does not deal with, for example, landing maneuvers or what to do if the unit detects a possible target on its way home.
[24]Nakashima and Noda 1998.

some behaviors are replaced or removed altogether, the context is updated and the whole agent behaves differently. If we apply this idea to our example, the result could appear as follows.

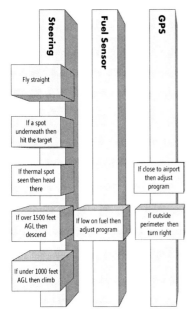 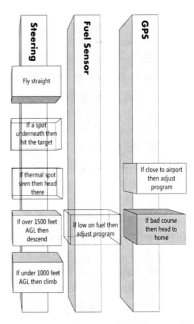

(a) There are three modules (sub-agents): Steering, Fuel Sensor, and GPS. Each of these represents an individual subsumption architecture and they operate simultaneously.

(b) Low fuel triggers the behavior of the Fuel Sensor, and so it reshuffles the configuration of the agent. The reaction on thermal spot in Steering module and the reaction on low fuel is removed (the first two would interfere with the new goal, returning to the base, and the latter is already superfluous). The behavior of keeping inside the operation perimeter in the GPS module is replaced by the behavior of keeping the right direction to the base.

Figure 3.4 – Example of dynamic subsumption architecture

Subagents (columns in dynamic subsumption) architecture work concurrently and independently of each other. Behaviors of one column are able to change behaviors in other cells and therefore "reconfigure" the program on the fly. In the aforementioned example, the agent works the same way as in the case of classical subsumption architecture until it is low on fuel. At that moment, the behavior of the fuel-sensor subagent reprograms the steering sub-agent, so that it is no longer primarily focused on searching for and eliminating targets, but on returning to the base. Actually, it is a moment when the agent is adjusting its goal.

Maes came up with another approach to constructing a reactive agent, so-called *Agent network architecture*.[25] The behaviors are not organized in layers, but in networks of interconnected modules. There are two types of module competence: action modules that perform certain actions when activated, and belief modules that hold beliefs or attitudes of the agent. Each module has a certain activation level – a real number that can rise or drop, depending on the module's inputs. This level of activation expresses how relevant the module is in the current context, or how probable its selection is. Each module has access to three lists: the list of conditions that have to be fulfilled in order to activate the respective module, and the add-list and delete-list where propositions (outputs) can be added. If output propositions of one module match input conditions of another, there is a successor link between these two modules. If the module is activated, the successor link amplifies the activation level of its successor module. For every successor link between modules, there is an inverse predecessor. If a module is not activated, it increases the activation level of its predecessor. It is a mechanism of spreading goals in the system. Besides that, there are conflictor links as well. They have the opposite function to the successor link: they inhibit the successor module.

The function of the system is driven by the signals from sensors and by goals that are sent to belief modules. Depending on the current situation, some of them get activated, some of them do not. The internal context of the entire agent is maintained this way. The more positive the signals (or the less negative the signals), the more reinforced is the current state of the agent. Activation of certain beliefs leads to the activation of the respective actions. Similarities between agent network architecture and neural networks are apparent. One can object that this approach is not purely reactive because the agents keep a certain representation of the external world in the states of their beliefs. On the other hand, there is no symbolic model of the environment and the intelligence of the agent is not intentional, but emerges from its interaction with the environment.

---

[25]Maes 1991.

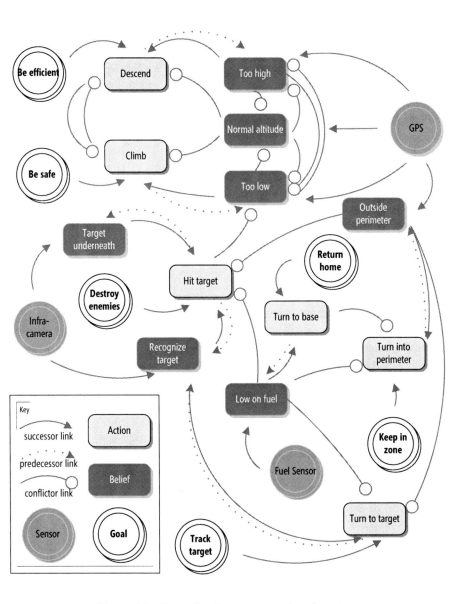

Figure 3.5 – Example of agent network architecture

Our example of a military system was transformed into the agent network architecture for comparison (see Figure 3.5 on page 37). The agent is composed of several functionalities. The altitude is maintained on the basis of signals from GPS in order to fulfill two goals: being safe (do not slam to ground, i.e., do not be too low), and being efficient (do not fly too high in order to save fuel and to be able to localize the target more easily). Signals are transformed into three beliefs: *too high* (corresponds with "be over 1500 feet" from our previous example), *too low* (under 1000 feet), and *normal altitude* (between these two limits). These beliefs are mutually contradictory, so there is a set of conflictor links among them, ensuring that the activity of one will be accompanied by the suppression of the others. If the camera sees a possible target, *recognize target* belief is reinforced. When the target is beneath the unit, the *hit target* action is triggered. It surpresses the too low belief herewith, so the agent does not stop its descent to 1000 feet. Next, there are two conflicting goals: *search targets* and *return home*. Normally, the former is prevailing, because it is reinforced by recognizing targets. When the unit runs out of fuel, it is overcome by the latter goal and the beliefs and actions that support searching targets start to be suppressed.

The agent network architecture is a very robust approach to the architecture of reactive agents. It can cover more complex modes of behavior and subtle relationships. On the other hand, the application of agent network architecture is much more intricate than in the case of subsumption architecture. It does not just mean a more demanding implementation, but also a more error-vulnerable code.

As demonstrated in this chapter, reactive agents are a robust and important paradigm of development of multi-agent systems. However, there is also a lot of criticism about this approach. First, because their function is mainly based on emergent properties that appear in a working system, it is very difficult to engineer and debug them for a specific task, or develop a general methodology for that purpose. It is mainly a matter of trial and error. Second, as reactive agents use information from their surroundings, they need an environment that can provide such information. Third, it is often simple to develop a system with a few behaviors; however, it can be very complicated, or even impossible, to develop agents with more layers and more sophisticated behavior where advanced interaction is necessary, especially when subsumption architecture is used.[26] Other kinds of architectures can mitigate this drawback. Fourth, although the system could work very effectively in certain conditions, it can be hard to adjust it for another environment. The entire system must be redesigned in that case. Fifth, except for experimental and scientific purposes, there are just a few application domains of reactive agents (games and agent-based simulations) nowadays.[27] Sixth, tasks that can be achieved are limited because of the

---

[26]Wooldridge 2002, p. 97.
[27]Nwana 1996.

lack of any cognition.[28] Finally, since the 90s, when the main body of reactive agent theory was published, there has been no intensive development in the field. It is often considered eccentric, and some agent-related textbooks (Shoham and Leyton-Brown's Multi-agent Systems[29] and Vidal's Fundamentals of Multiagent Systems[30]) do not deal with it at all. From the author's point of view, purely reactive agents should not be ignored because there are several very sound ideas behind them that people interested in multi-agent systems should know and understand. Moreover, in designing agent-based simulations, purely reactive agents are often a good choice, due to their simplicity, performance, and applicability. Their apparent limitations can be overcome using more advanced architectures and with the combination of deliberative agent traits in so-called *hybrid agents* (see section 3.5).

---

[28]Jung, Cheng, and Zelinsky 1998.
[29]Shoham and Leyton-Brown 2009.
[30]Vidal 2006.

3.4   Deliberative Agents

Deliberative agents (they are also often called *intelligent agents, rational agents,* and other names) represent an important multi-agent paradigm. The agents are inherently intelligent, they store a representation of the outer world in their memory, and they make decisions about their future actions on the basis of that memory. There are more approaches to the implementation of intelligence in deliberative agents, but in all cases, the intelligent behavior is embedded in the sole agents, unlike the reactive agents where the source of intelligence is in the interaction with the environment. The way that deliberative agents reason is closer to human intelligence than that of reactive agents.

The deliberative agents are able to pursue complex and long-term goals; they can maintain a whole hierarchy of goals and choose those that are the most appropriate in the moment. They can coordinate their conduct with other agents in order to reach objectives that they cannot manage alone. If an agent faces a task that it cannot accomplish, it can ask other agents for cooperation. They can accept or reject the request, depending on their own objectives. The agents can form coalitions in order to reach their goals as a group (albeit it is not very common, because multi-agent tasks with a chance for any synergic effect are rare[31]). They can also bargain and close contracts in order to resolve conflicting objectives. The knowledge that the deliberative agents bear is not given. They can learn from their past experiences (and even from the experience of other agents under some circumstances) and improve their skills over time.

As described above, deliberative agents are theoretically a very powerful and robust concept. In agent-based simulations, they can mimic various considerable human traits. On the other hand, their main disadvantage is their complexity. It is very hard to develop a deliberative agent that includes the properties mentioned above. Such agents require advanced artificial intelligence and hence, they are very computational-power intensive and vulnerable to errors, due to their complexity.

As defined above, agents receive percepts and communication inputs from their surroundings and perform actions that, on the other hand, influence their environment. But what happens inside a deliberative agent?

Generally, the inputs are transformed into the outputs by a certain reasoning mechanism. It could be based on various principles (as will be discussed further); it could be more or less sophisticated, but it will probably always involve the agent's memory as the storage of the agent's context (including its knowledge and its "present state") and its goals that steer its decision making. This arrangement corresponds to Russell and Norvig's *goal-based agents.*[32,33] In Figure 3.6 there is a scheme of a

---

[31] Vidal 2006, p. 50.

[32] Russell and Norvig 1995, pp. 42–44.

[33] They also suggest the utility-based agent as an even more advanced form of agent architecture, but from the author's point of view, utility-based agent is only a specific kind of agent's implementation.

deliberative agent as an extension of the scheme in Figure 3.1 on page 25 (adapted from Wooldridge[34]).

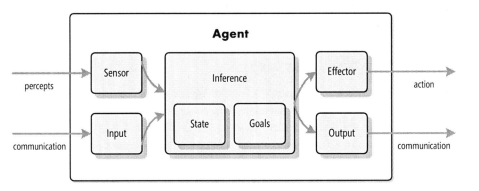

Figure 3.6 – Scheme of the architecture of the deliberative agent. On input, there is sensory perception of the environment and received communication from other agents. The input is processed in an inference mechanism that should make a decision about what to do. Input has an impact on the current state of the agent that, along with the agent's goals, constitutes a background for future decisions. The decisions are then materialized by the agent's effectors as its action, or by communication interface as its output.

In the first step, *input* function converts percepts and incoming communication from outside of the agent into the internal symbolic representation of input:

$$input : E \rightarrow Inp, \qquad (3.4)$$

where E is the environment and Inp is the input.

Next, *process* function updates the agent's context (internal state) according the input:

$$process : Inp \times S \rightarrow S, \qquad (3.5)$$

where S is the context.

And finally, *action* function performs the action of the agent based on the current state:

$$action : S \rightarrow Ac, \qquad (3.6)$$

where Ac denotes the action (it could be either physical action or outgoing communication to other agents). If we compare Figure 3.6 and the above mentioned functions, we will see that there are no goals in the formulas. Actually, they are incorporated in the *action* function that generates the decision, based on the internal state and current goals.

---

[34]Wooldridge 2002, p. 36.

Mentioned above is a general description of the scheme of deliberative agents. Most deliberative agents encompass similar architecture, but they differ in implementation, architecture, and the complexity of the individual modules, especially the inference mechanism of the action function. In the following sections, several approaches to their design will be discussed.

3.4.1   Utility-based approach

An important approach to designing deliberative agents is based on *utility theory*. Utility theory is a crucial concept upon which modern economics is based. Due to its importance in economics, the accompanying theory is deeply elaborated, and theory of agency can, hence, draw from a huge body of relevant knowledge. Because our primary application domain involves social and economical simulations, this approach is indeed even more relevant for us.

Utility is a "measure of satisfaction." The more utility the agent expects from a certain action, the more desirable the action that could bring it is. Or the higher the utility, the closer the agent is to its goal. In contemporary economics, there are two basic approaches to comprehending utility:[35]

Cardinal utility is measurable. Any action turns into a certain amount of utility represented, for example, by a real number, and therefore, utility is a quantity just like, for instance, a physical property. Unfortunately, this concept leads to numerous practical problems such as a problem of interpersonal comparability of utility. Everybody has his or her own utility scale that is incomparable with the utility scales of others, as nobody can look inside the other's head and find out what he or she thinks. Suppose a charity that resolves who should receive an amount of aid (let's say that it is indivisible). Two people pursue the aid, and both will probably say that they deserve it more than the other, because it has a greater value (or utility) for them. If there are no objective criteria to compare their situation, there is no general way to enumerate their utilities and decide who "deserves" it more. Hence, cardinal utility theory in economics is typically deemed obsolete by most of schools of thought.

In *ordinal utility* theory, the utility is not measurable, but only comparable. Everybody can easily say what option he or she prefers before the other one. Interpersonal comparability still is not possible, but preferences could be expressed interpersonally during exchange. If people willingly decide to change one good for another (or for money), they surely value the good more than the amount of money. Ordinal utility then is no measure, but just a succession of preferences. There is no doubt that for practical application in computing, cardinal utility is more suitable, because while working with real numbers is simple, processing of sequences of preferences is impractical. We must however remember limitation of this approach.

---

[35]Soukupová et al. 2003, pp. 51–53.

The utility-based agent[36] makes decisions in order to maximize its expected utility that can be enumerated by a real number. There is *utility function* in the agent's inference (action) function that maps the possible states of the world to the real number:

$$u : O \rightarrow \Re, \tag{3.7}$$

where O is a set of options that represent the final states of the world that the agent can reach.

The agent chooses the state where it expects the highest outcome. This situation is rather simple when the agent's sensors provide perfect and unbiased information, and the agent's action will always lead exactly to the state that the agent expects (in other words, in case the agent's environment is accessible and deterministic – see section 3.1). This is normally not the case. The options are what the agent perceives, and hence, they may not be real possibilities. The percept could be biased (agent sensors need not be perfect) and the reality can change during the agent's reasoning. Suppose the agent knows the probability of reaching state $s_{t+1} \in O$ when it is in state s and takes action a. This probability is returned by function $T(s_t, a, s_{t+1})$ that we call *transition function*.[37] It is apparent that:

$$\sum_{s_{t+1} \in O} T(s_t, a, s_{t+1}) = 1. \tag{3.8}$$

The *expected utility* of action a in state s is as follows:

$$E[s_t, a, u] = \sum_{s_{t+1} \in O} T(s_t, a, s_{t+1}) u(s_{t+1}), \tag{3.9}$$

where $u(s_{t+1})$ is the utility of reaching state s_{t+1}. It means the expected utility of taking action a, when the agent is in state s. The agent indeed chooses the action a that maximizes the expected utility in the respective state. Formally:

$$\max_{a \in A}(E[s_t, a, u]). \tag{3.10}$$

A suitable model for the description of the agent's behavior is Markov Decision Processes (MDP), a mathematical framework named after Andrey Markov for modeling decision-making in cases when results are partly random and partly under the control of the decision maker.

Optimal policy is the action from the set of all possible actions that agent can do in a certain situation that leads to the highest expected utility:

$$\pi(s_t) = a \in A; \max_a(E[s_t, a, u]) \tag{3.11}$$

or

$$\pi(s_t) = \arg\max_a(E[s_t, a, u]). \tag{3.12}$$

---

[36]Russell and Norvig 1995, p. 44.
[37]Vidal 2006, p. 11.

Expected reward is the expected utility that the agent gains in the next step given to its present situation when it makes the best possible action:

$$R(s_{t+1}) = \max_{a}(E\,[s_t, a, u]).\qquad(3.13)$$

If we can choose whether to get the same reward in time t or in time $t + 1$, it is rational to choose time t, because our future is always uncertain and we never know what happens until time $t + 1$ and if we will even still exist. Therefore, in spite of the same nominal amount, for correct intertemporal comparison, the future reward should be discounted by a certain discount factor γ that expresses uncertainty. Factor γ is from (0;1).

$$u(s) = R(s_t) + \gamma\,R(s_{t+1})\qquad(3.14)$$

Theoretically, the concept of utility-based agents is simple and straightforward. Unfortunately, its practical application brings numerous obstacles. First, in reality, the utility valuation of possible states of the world is a complex problem. The same goes for the enumeration of probabilities of reaching individual states, discount factors, and actually all other variables in the model. Second, the solution of the equations could be relatively slow, due to their nonlinear character. And finally, the approach does not handle multiple goals, especially if short-term and long-term goals collide.

"There is no such thing as a free lunch."[38] For any utility gain, the agent needs to expend some costs, and only if the utility obtained exceeds the cost spent, the agent will be better off. Therefore, we should introduce a cost function for any possible state as an offset of the utility function. For simplicity, however, if not stated otherwise, we will calculate with net utility (i.e., the utility after deduction of costs necessary to reach it). It could be indeed either positive or negative, depending on whether the agent is better or worse off.

This is a good point to introduce a simple example: suppose an agent is in city A and needs to get to city B for an important business meeting. It can choose from three means of transportation: car, train, or bus.

Driving a car is relatively comfortable and relatively fast, but expensive, as the agent travels alone. Unfortunately, the agent is not a good navigator and it can get lost, which would mean missing the meeting by getting there too late, and also driving for a longer time, for a greater distance, and consuming much more fuel on the way. Traveling on a train is very comfortable, but slow, because there is no direct service between A and B, and the train could be late. The cost is between the cost for driving a car and traveling by bus. The bus is the cheapest alternative; it will be almost surely on time, but it is very uncomfortable, and there is only one bus between A and B daily with departure at an inconvenient time. It would mean the agent would have to leave much earlier and spend almost twice the time on the journey than it would by car or train.

---

[38]Milton Friedman

Let's say the cost of traveling by car is 15, the cost by train is 10, and the cost by bus is 5. The utility coming from the comfort of the respective means of transport is 10 for the train, 7 for the car and 3 for the bus. Hence, the net utility of traveling (u_t) by car, train, and bus is -8, 0, and -2, respectively. The utilities of the possible results (u_r) of the agent are 10 if it stays at home (and makes, for example, a phone call instead of going to the meeting), 50 when it gets to the destination on time, 40 when it gets there too early, 30 when it gets there too late, and -20 when it gets lost (then neither the meeting or the call is possible – there is no cellular coverage in deep forests, and the business is lost). In fact, the agent is on a different level of utility when it arrives on time on the bus (48), or on the train (50), or by car (42), and each of these situations is a separate state. Let staying home and doing nothing be the utility of 0. For simplicity, there are just the utilities of results depicted in Figure 3.7, but we need to calculate all possibilities (i.e., with 9 states). The total utility of the respective state is denoted u.

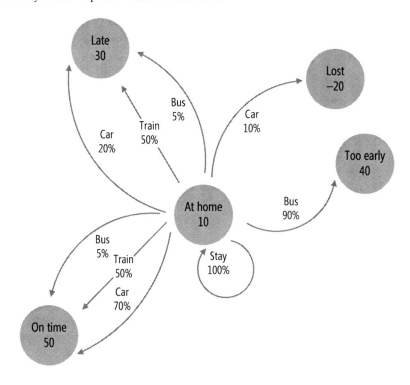

Figure 3.7 – Scheme of the Markov decision process of traveler.

The values of the transition function are in Table 3.1 on page 46 and in the Table 3.2. There are expected utilities of the particular agent's actions (we can consider $\gamma = 1$, because we think about one round only).

Table 3.1 – The expected utilities for the results of the individual agent's actions. Utility adjustments for using the specific means of transport are not incorporated.

s_t	a	s_{t+1}	T
At home	Bus	On time	5%
At home	Train	On time	50%
At home	Car	On time	70%
At home	Bus	Late	5%
At home	Train	Late	50%
At home	Car	Late	20%
At home	Car	Lost	10%
At home	Bus	Too early	90%
At home	Stay	At home	100%

Table 3.2 – Calculation of expected utilities of the agent's possible actions.

s_t	a	s_{t+1}	T	u_r	u_t	u	$T_x u_x$	E_a
At home	Bus	On time	5%	50	-2	48	2.4	
At home	Bus	Late	5%	30	-2	28	1.4	38
At home	Bus	Too early	90%	40	-2	38	34.2	
At home	Car	On time	70%	50	-8	42	29.4	
At home	Car	Late	20%	30	-8	22	4.4	31
At home	Car	Lost	10%	-20	-8	-28	-2.8	
At home	Train	On time	50%	50	0	50	25.0	40
At home	Train	Late	50%	30	0	30	15.0	
At home	Stay	At home	100%	10	0	10	10.0	10

It is obvious that on the basis of the above calculation, the agent's optimal policy is to *go by train*. Calculation of the optimal policy is not difficult and even if there were more decision rounds, the complexity of the task would still be acceptable. The main problem for development of such an agent is how it would estimate the utilities and probabilities of the particular situations if they were not preset.

3.4.2 Logic-based approach

A logic-based approach is the concept of agency that comes from symbolic artificial intelligence and is based on logical deduction over a set of known statements.[39] Simply said, the agent holds the information about the world in its memory (or knowledge base,

[39]Wooldridge 2002, p. 47.

in artificial-intelligence terminology), let's say in predicates of first-order logic or Prolog facts. The agent's inference mechanism (*action* function) has a set of *deduction rules*. These are logical rules that can be applied to facts.

The reasoning process works as follows (adapted from Wooldridge[40]). Let S be a set of logical formulae that represent the agent's state. Let $\sigma \in S$ be a single logical formula as a part of agent's state. Let ρ be a set of deduction rules that the agent uses to derive its decisions. We write $\sigma \vdash_\rho \varphi$ if φ can be derived from σ using decision rules ρ.

Let Ac be a set of all possible actions that the agent can do and $\alpha \in Ac$ be a single action. The agent picks one predicate from S after another and it tries to deduce $Do(\alpha)$ for each $\alpha \in Ac$. If it succeeds, α is returned as a proper action that should be done in the moment and the reasoning process ends. If there is no α that leads to a solution, we can broaden the specification and try to find α such that $Do(\alpha)$ is not contradictory to σ; that is, an action that is not explicitly prohibited. Formally: $\sigma \nvdash_\rho \neg Do(\alpha)$. If there is even no such action, *do nothing* is returned. There is an example of pseudocode of the *action* function based on the above-mentioned algorithm in Figure 3.8.

```
1: function ACTION(σ)
2:     for all α ∈ Ac do
3:         if σ ⊢ρ Do(α) then
4:             return α
5:         end if
6:     end for
7:     for all α ∈ Ac do
8:         if σ ⊬ρ ¬Do(α) then
9:             return α
10:        end if
11:    end for
12:    return do nothing
13: end function
```

Figure 3.8 – Pseudocode of *action* function of theorem-proving agent

It is a good place for an example. In future, robots perhaps overtake more of human work. Suppose a robot (let's call it *Stockkeeper*) that monitors shelves in a store and its duty is restocking them when the wares are sold out. In our example, a robot has just few shelves in care with only two kinds of goods: grease and shovels. The robot monitors the shelves and if an amount of a particular good falls under a limit that the robot keeps in its memory, it has to trundle to a storeroom, pick the proper good and replenish the shelf.

---

[40]Ibid., p. 49.

The set of deduction rules (ρ) is in Listing 3.1.[41]

Listing 3.1 – Rule set of *Stockkeeper* robot (Prolog)

```
1  lack:-minstock(A,X),inshelf(A,Y),X>Y.
2  do(go_to_storeroom):-once(lack),position(shopfloor),\+ carry(_).
3  do(pickup_wares)    :-once(lack),position(storeroom),\+ carry(_).
4  do(go_to_shopfloor):-once(lack),position(storeroom),once(carry(_)).
5  do(put_wares)       :-position(shopfloor),once(carry(_)).
```

Agent's database S consists of several facts that are updated continuously by the *process* function. The example of S is in Listing 3.2.

Listing 3.2 – An example of the set of facts in *Stockkeeper*'s knowledge base (Prolog)

```
1  minstock(shovel,3).
2  minstock(grease,40).
3  inshelf(shovel,2).
4  inshelf(grease,20).
5  position(shopfloor).
```

Stockkeeper knows that the minimum level in shelves is 3 in the case of shovels and 40 in the case of grease (it is a permanent knowledge that could be updated time to time only, when, for example, shelf dispositions are being revised due to changes in seasonal demand). The agent also knows that there are 2 shovels and 20 packages of grease on the shelf. It is an immediate knowledge. Agent's camera saw it, the *input* function transformed this percept into the symbolic form and the *process* function entered it into S. Finally, the agent knows its position – it stands in the shop (and not, for example, outside the building or in the storage area). If the robot's sensors register any new relevant percept, the knowledge base is updated accordingly.

Function *action* browses the set S continually and tries to derive a Do theorem for some α. With the fact-set in Listing 3.2 theorem `lack` holds and so `once(lack)` holds as well, `position(shopfloor)` is valid and there is no `carry` fact. It implies `do(go_to_storeroom)` can be derived from the aforementioned facts. It is easy to verify that there cannot be inferred Do for any other α from S shown in Listing 3.2.

When the robot moves to the storeroom, its sensors detect it and `position(shopfloor)` is replaced with `position(storeroom)` fact. It causes `do(go_to_storeroom)` cannot be derived anymore and `do(pickup_wares)` is deduced instead. Robot picks wanted goods, which means that `carry(shovel)` or `carry(grease)` are included into S. It implies the deduction of `do(go_to_shopfloor)` where `position(storeroom)` is removed and `position(shopfloor)` is included into the knowledge base which leads to the inference of `do(put_wares)` theorem. The carried goods are offloaded what leads to

---

[41]Prolog program code is used for the demonstration, because it could be immediately compiled and verified. Its eventual transformation into formal logic notation is more or less straightforward.

the update of `inshelf` facts and removing of `carry` facts. In that moment, no *Do* predicate can be derived and so the agent does nothing and waits until its cameras detect a shortage of a certain good.

The system in our example would probably work fine. However, in reality we have seldom such ideal, laboratory conditions. The robot must deal with – among other things – a much more complex situation, ambiguous percepts or even contradictory facts. Even such a subtle change of the situation could bring serious problems.

Let's improve the program in the way that the robot does not go generally to a "storeroom," but directly to a shelf or pile with the specific good it wants to take. The adjusted Prolog program is in Listing 3.3 (note that this relatively simple improvement required 60% more lines of code and the solution is far from being perfect, as discussed below).

Listing 3.3 – Rule set of *Stockkeeper* robot. The location of goods is distinguished. (Prolog)

```
lack(A):-minstock(A,X),inshelf(A,Y),X>Y.
position(storeroom):-position(shovels).
position(storeroom):-position(grease).
do(go_to_shovels):-lack(shovel),\+ position(shovels),\+ carry(shovel).
do(go_to_grease):-lack(grease),\+ position(grease),\+ carry(grease).
do(pickup_wares):-once(lack(_)),position(storeroom),\+ carry(_).
do(go_to_shopfloor):-once(lack(_)),position(storeroom),once(carry(_)).
do(put_wares):-position(shopfloor),once(carry(_)).
```

One of the biggest obstacles for the implementation of logic based agents seems to be the situation when a *Do* predicate is derived for multiple α. Using the *action* function from Figure 3.8 on page 47 there is no way to find the optimal solution. The function will simply perform the first valid *Do* it gets. It means that the behavior of the agent can be unpredictable. Using the code in Listing 3.3, there can occur more such situations. For instance, do(`go_to_grease`) and do(`go_to_shovels`) can hold simultaneously and the robot can then behave randomly in the moment. Nevertheless, it is not the worst case, because it could still work well. The worst situation is when do(`go_to_shovels`) and both do(`go_to_shopfloor`) hold together, which can lead to a chaotic behavior of the robot and even to a deadlock.

The aforementioned problem is not a flaw of the particular design of the *action* function, but a drawback of Boolean logic where statements could be either true or false and all are equally true or equally false, so we have no instrument to distinguish which action is "more true" or more appropriate in the moment. The only possible solution is to construct the inference rules in such a manner that the possible solutions are fully *disjoint*; that is, there are no two valid *Do* predicates for two different actions in the same moment. Formally:

$$\forall\alpha\forall\beta\forall\sigma(\neg(\sigma\vdash_\rho Do(\alpha) \wedge \sigma\vdash_\rho Do(\beta) \wedge \alpha\neq\beta)); \alpha,\beta\in Ac,\sigma\in S. \qquad (3.15)$$

Let the ρ set that fulfills the conditions according to Equation 3.15 be called a *disjoint rule set* and we will use *conjoint rule sets* for all other kinds of rule sets.

For more complex tasks, developing and debugging of sound and disjoint rule sets could be extremely difficult and the intricacy of inference rules could be substantial. We can achieve better results with the implementation of *fuzzy logic*.[42] Predicates in fuzzy logic are not either true or false, but they can have assigned more levels of truth. In our example we use a predicate `lack/1` to determine if there is a lack of a certain good. It seems that in this case, there is no doubt whether there is or is not a lack of something when we know the required minimum stock and the immediate number of the stock on the shelf. However, when for example the minimum of grease is 40 packages and there are 39 packages on shelf, they should be restocked, but in fact it is no big deal – there are still enough wares to sell. When there are just 10 packages, it is more likely that they will be sold-out soon and the replenishment is more urgent. If there are no packages at all, their delivery is critical, otherwise the customers will be disappointed. On the other hand, when there are 42 packages, it is not necessary to restock grease immediately; however, it is probable that it will be in the near future, so it is not a bad idea to go to the storeroom. And finally, if there are 200 packages, it is obvious that no refills are needed at all. Any level of truth in fuzzy logic can have assigned a word and we call it a *linguistic variable*. It can consist of the mere fuzzy predicate (e.g., true, false) and fuzzy modifier (very, probably, almost, etc).

The set of all possible levels of validity of the fuzzy predicate (the so called *grade of membership*) we call *fuzzy set*. Let N be a fuzzy set. The membership degree of x in the set N is defined by so-called membership function π. Usually, the range of a membership function is $\langle 0; 1 \rangle$. For instance, if there are a minimum 40 packages as a required amount of grease, and there are just 2 packages on shelf, then `lack(grease)` will be absolutely true with the value of membership function of 1. When there are 39 packages on the shelf, the grade of membership could be quite true with the value of π let's say 0.6, with 42 packages it could be almost true with π of 0.4, and so on. The membership function could be indeed either discrete or continuous.[43]

In order to work with fuzzy logic we should define fuzzy operators.[44] Let X and Y be fuzzy variables. Then:

1 The *negation* is the set theoretic complement, i.e., $\neg X \equiv 1 - \pi(X)$

2 The *disjunction* is the set theoretic union, i.e., $X \vee Y \equiv \max(\pi(X); \pi(Y))$

3 The *conjunction* is the set theoretic intersection, i.e., $X \wedge Y \equiv \min(\pi(X); \pi(Y))$

---

[42]Zadeh 1988.

[43]Ibid.

[44]For lucidity, in order to distinguish fuzzy operators from the classical Boolean ones, the fuzzy operators will be typeset in **bold**.

Besides the classical operators we also use $\vdash$ operator in fuzzy version. We write $\sigma \vdash_\rho \varphi$ if φ can be derived from σ using decision rules ρ with a certain level of validity. For using fuzzy logic, we indeed need to modify the *action* function. Now the situation is much more intricate, because even the validity of the *Do* predicate is fuzzy. One way is to find such opt_α for all $\alpha \in Ac$ that $\pi Do(\alpha)$ is maximum, formally:

$$opt_\alpha(\sigma) = \max \pi(\sigma \vdash_\rho Do(\alpha)); \alpha \in Ac, \quad (3.16)$$

nonetheless it could lead to finding of a very low opt_α (let's say 0.1) that is however still the highest of all possible. Hence we must set the minimum level of membership function ξ that we can treat as a threshold level. If opt_α will remain below ξ, *action* function returns *do nothing*.

A possible concept of fuzzy *action* function is shown in Figure 3.9.

```
1: function ACTION(σ)
2:     optα ← 0
3:     for all α ∈ Ac do
4:         if π(σ ⊢ρ Do(α)) > optα then
5:             a ← α
6:             optα ← π(σ ⊢ρ Do(α))
7:         end if
8:     end for
9:     if optα ≥ ξ then
10:         return a
11:    else
12:        return do nothing
13:    end if
14: end function
```

Figure 3.9 – Pseudocode of fuzzy *action* function of theorem-proving agent with fuzzy logic

The fuzzy concept means a better solution of the logic-based agent. Using fuzzy logic, inference rules can be simpler as the avoidance of conjoint rules need not be solved explicitly. On the other hand, even with fuzzy logic there is no guarantee that there will be only one solution, that is that for certain σ there will be only one $Do(\alpha)$ with the highest value of π function. If there are two or more $Do(\alpha)$ with the maximum of π function, *action* function will actually return a random one from them. Nevertheless, it still seems that this situation is less likely than while using classical Boolean logic and that there is a lower chance that the results will be contradictory.

Unfortunately, there are many serious problems with the implementation of agents based on the logic approach. First, the transformation of the states of the world into the logical facts (so called *transduction*) is a very complex problem. It was difficult even in the case of aforementioned utility-based agents, but in logic-based agents it is perhaps even trickier. Second, computational capacity requirements could be huge due to the severity of processing logical rules and there is no guarantee that any solution will be always reached. Third, in dynamic environments, any practical implementation of logic-based agents will be time-constrained, because the speed of their reasoning must be adequate to the pace that the environment is changing.[45] Fourth, the logic-based approach is vulnerable to logical contradictions that often mean that the inference mechanism does not lead to a single solution. Using fuzzy logic, this problem can be reduced but not entirely removed. Otherwise some additional conflict-solving technique must be implemented. And finally, developing and debugging complex and sound logic rules is tremendously difficult and so impractical for real application.

3.4.3 BDI approach

BDI stands for *belief-desire-intention* and it is one of the best known and most widespread agency approaches with dozens of implementations of practical reasoning systems based on BDI architecture and well-developed underpinning theory.[46] In our typology, it is actually just an extended case of the logic-based approach with a more sophisticated reasoning algorithm than, for example, the one introduced in Figure 3.6 on page 41. However, the importance of BDI in the theory of agency and its recognition in the multi-agent community requires a special concern for this topic.

The approach has its roots in cognitive sciences and comes from a model of human reasoning that was developed by Michael Bratman.[47] According to Wooldridge[48] BDI combines three components:

- *philosophical component* – based on the model of human rational action by Bratman

- *software architecture component* – although the model does not prescribe any specific implementation, it was successfully implemented many times (PRS, dMARS, JAM,[49] JADEX,[50] JASON,[51] JACK,[52] 3APL,[53] among many others[54]) and used for real-world applications

---

[45]Wooldridge 2002, p. 54.
[46]Georgeff et al. 1999.
[47]Bratman 1999.
[48]Wooldridge 2000, p. 21.
[49]See http://www.marcush.net/IRS (visited on 23.7.2009)
[50]See http://jadex.informatik.uni-hamburg.de (visited on 23.7.2009)
[51]See http://jason.sourceforge.net (visited on 23.7.2009)
[52]See http://www.aosgrp.com.au/products/jack (visited on 23.7.2009)
[53]See http://www.cs.uu.nl/3apl (visited on 23.7.2009)
[54]See chapter B.

- *logical component* – key aspects of BDI are represented as a set of logical axioms and logical rules. BDI formal logics is well established and widely used in the theory of agency.

According to the BDI model, beliefs, desires and intentions are key steps of rational action. *Belief* represents knowledge of the agent. *Belief set* means a set of beliefs; that is, a knowledge base where the agent holds information about the environment, other agents and itself. The reason why pieces of knowledge are called beliefs in this model is that the agent's perception may not be reliable and so the autonomous agent cannot always work with proper states of environment as long as it can be never sure that they are true. The agent's knowledge can be incomplete or incorrect. Therefore the agent works with beliefs, that is with the information it believes it is true. In most cases there is no substantial difference between belief and knowledge (at least for a developer of a BDI agent).

Desire is what the agent wants to do. The agent has a set of desires that represent a set of actions that the agent wants to achieve, both realistic and unrealistic (in a given context) or even conflicting. An agent can want to work on one task and on another one (and on a dozen other things) in the same moment. Of course, in reality it has to choose just some of these things, regarding its capacity. Then desires turn into *intentions*. Intentions are committed desires and of course, just a part of desires can turn into intentions, as just a part of desires can be achieved.[55] Commitment to certain intention is not forever, of course. If the intention cannot be achieved anymore (e.g., agent wants to win an auction, but another agents bids over the first agent's budget), it becomes obsolete (agent leaves its concern for the intention), there are other, at least partially conflicting intentions with a higher priority (constrained resources) or the agent simply gives up its effort after several fruitless attempts, the commitment could cease. In implementation of BDI agents, a right level of commitment could be sometimes an issue, as agents could be undercommitted (abandon their intentions too early) or overcommitted (do not give it up even if they ought to).[56] The purpose of intentions is to constrain the agent's reasoning, as the agent cannot do more actions than what its resources allow.

Intention is typically realized through a plan. The BDI model does not solve planning specifically; however, in most implementations, agents include a *plan library*, which is a base of plans for all possible intentions. The agent continually updates its beliefs according to percepts and incoming communication (input is processed through a *Belief Resolution Function* – BRF and stored into a belief set). In every round the agent seeks desires that can be invoked according to its present set of beliefs. The desire pool is then a source from which the agent picks (filters) desires to fulfill. They become intentions and agents will execute them using a specific plan. All these stages can run concurrently;

---

[55] Wooldridge 2000, p. 7.
[56] Wooldridge 2002, p. 77.

for example, the agent's beliefs are updated while it is executing a plan, which corresponds with human conduct. In Figure 3.10, there is a scheme of an agent based on BDI architecture.[57]

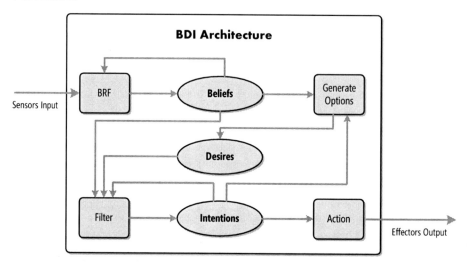

Figure 3.10 – Scheme of the architecture of a BDI agent. Sensory input is processed through the BRF function and new beliefs are stored. Desires are derived from actual beliefs in the Generate Options function. From desires, intentions are filtered and they are performed by the action function.

As mentioned above, unlike most of other agency matters, BDI was successfully implemented many times. *AgentSpeak(L)* language became one of its best known implementations. AgentSpeak(L) is an agent-oriented programming language that was developed by Anand Rao, it is based on a restricted first-order language with events and actions and is similar to Prolog to some extent.[58] BDI architecture will be demonstrated using AgentSpeak(L) in the following text. Other BDI implementations can use various language syntaxes and can be somewhat different, although the basic principles indeed stay the same.

An AgentSpeak(L) agent contains a set of *base beliefs* and a set of plans. A *belief atom* is a first-order predicate, and belief atoms or their negations are called *belief literals*. An initial set of beliefs is a collection of basic belief atoms.[59]

AgentSpeak(L) uses two kinds of goals: achievement goals and test goals. *Achievement goals* are predicates (as for beliefs) prefixed with operators '!'. *Test goals* begin with '?'. Achievement goals mean that the agent wants to achieve a state of the world where

[57] Wooldridge 2002.
[58] Rao 1996.
[59] Bordini and Hübner 2007, p. 2.

its predicate is true. On the other hand, test goals return a unification for the associated predicate with one of the agent's beliefs; it fails if no unification is found. A *triggering event* defines which events may start the execution of a plan. There are two types of triggering events: those related to the addition ('+') and deletion ('−') of beliefs or goals. The AgentSpeak(L) interpreter also runs a set of *events* and a set of *intentions*, and it requires three *selection functions*. The *event selection function* selects one of the set of events; the *option selection function* selects an applicable plan from a set of plans; and an *intention selection function* selects one particular intention from the set of intentions. The selection functions are supposed to be agent-specific; that is, they should make selections based on an agent's characteristics.[60]

Intentions are particular courses of action which the agent has committed in order to reach certain goals. Each intention represents a number of partially instantiated plans. Events, that may initiate the execution of plans can be *external* when coming from the perception of the agent's environment (i.e., addition and deletion of beliefs based on perception are external events); or *internal* when generated from the agent's own execution of a plan (i.e., a subgoal in a plan generates an event of type "addition of achievement goal"). In the latter case, the event is accompanied with the intention that has it generated. External events create new intentions, representing separate focuses of attention for the agent's acting on the environment.

Every interpretation cycle of an agent program, AgentSpeak(L) updates a list of events that may be generated from the perception of the environment or from the execution of intentions (when subgoals are specified in the bodies of plans). It is assumed that beliefs are updated from perception and every time there are changes in the agent's beliefs, it leads to the insertion of an event in the set of events. This belief revision function is not a part of the AgentSpeak(L) interpreter, but rather a necessary component of the agent architecture.

After the event selection function has selected an event, AgentSpeak(L) has to unify that event with triggering events of the plans. It generates a set of all relevant plans. By checking whether the context part of the plans falls in line with the agent's beliefs, AgentSpeak(L) determines a set of applicable plans (plans that can actually be used at that moment for handling the chosen event). Then the option selection function chooses a single applicable plan from that set, which becomes the intended means for handling that event, and either moves that plan on the top of an existing intention (if the event was an internal one), or creates a new intention in the set of intentions (if the event was external, i.e., generated from perception of the environment).[61]

The last step in this stage is a selection of a single intention to be executed in that cycle. The intention selection function selects one of the agent's intentions (i.e., one of the independent stacks of partially instantiated plans within the set of intentions). On

---

[60]Ibid., p. 3.
[61]Ibid., p. 4.

the top of that intention there is a plan, and the formula in the beginning of its body is taken for execution. This implies that either a basic action is performed by the agent on its environment, an internal event is generated (in case the selected formula is an achievement goal), or a test goal is performed (which means that the set of beliefs has to be checked).

If the intention is to perform a basic action or a test goal, the set of intentions needs to be updated. In the case of a test goal, the belief base will be searched for a belief atom that unifies with the predicate in the test goal. If that search succeeds, the test goal is removed from the intention from which it was taken and the plan itself is executed further according to the test goal. When a basic action is selected, the necessary updating of the set of intentions is simply to remove that action from the intention. When all formulae in the body of a plan have been removed (i.e., they have been executed), the whole plan is removed from the intention, and so is the achievement goal that generated it. This ends the cycle of execution, and AgentSpeak(L) starts over again, checking the state of the environment after agents have acted upon it, generating the relevant events, and so forth.[62]

This is a good place to introduce an example. There are sources of two very simple agents in Listings 3.5 and 3.4 written in AgentSpeak(L) for Jason. The agents are Buyer and Seller, they contain a simple negotiation protocol and their purpose is to make a deal.

Listing 3.4 – Code of Buyer Agent. (AgentSpeak(L))

```
1   /* Initial beliefs and rules */
2
3   require(gas).
4   maxprice(gas,25).
5
6   /* Initial goals */
7
8   !byuGasoline.
9
10  /* Plans */
11
12  +!byuGasoline : true <-
13          .send(seller,tell,hello).
14
15  +hello[source(seller)] : require(Ware) <-
16          .send(seller,tell,require(Ware)).
17
18  +price(Ware, OfferedPrice)[source(S)] :
19          maxprice(Ware, Price) & Price < OfferedPrice  <-
20          .send(seller,untell,require(Ware)).
21
22  +price(Ware, OfferedPrice)[source(S)] :
23          not (maxprice(Ware, Price) & Price < OfferedPrice) <-
24          .send(seller,tell,buy(Ware)).
```

---

[62]Bordini and Hübner 2007, pp. 4–5.

The buyer agent's initial beliefs are `require(gas)` and `maxprice(gas,25)`, which means that the agent needs to buy some gas and the maximum price it is willing to pay is 25. The agent has only one goal: to buy gasoline (line 8). It is a simple situation, because the agent's reasoning is relatively straightforward. The database of plans consists of several plans that will be discussed further.

The plan for `!buyGasoline` is an unconditional plan and its only action is to send hello to the Seller Agent. Hello is a simple belief that represents the beginning of negotiation. Let's interrupt the description of Buyer here for the moment and take a look at Seller.

Listing 3.5 – Code of Seller Agent. (AgentSpeak(L))

```
/* Initial beliefs and rules */

instock(gas).
price(gas,30).

/* Initial goals */

/* Plans */

+hello[source(S)] <-
        .send(S,tell,hello).

+require(Ware)[source(S)] : instock(Ware) <-
        !offer(S,Ware).

-require(Ware)[source(S)] : offered(S,Ware) <-
        -offered(S,Ware).

+!offer(S,Ware) : true <-
        +offered(S,Ware);
        ?price(Ware,Price);
        .send(S,tell,price(Ware,Price)).
```

Seller has two initial beliefs as well: `instock(gas)`, meaning that gasoline is in stock (information about the quantity would be perhaps more useful, but let's keep things simple) and `price(gas,30)`, meaning that the price of the gas is 30. Seller has no initial goals, but it has several plans that should react to various events. The first event that is probably received by Seller arises when `hello` comes from Buyer and is added into Seller's belief set (line 10, Listing 3.5). The agent's reply is a `hello` belief as well (note that Seller does not send it to Buyer, but the S variable is used instead, so the agent would communicate with anybody, not just with Buyer). What would happen, if there was an error in code and the body of this plan contained the same content as the Seller's plan? One would guess that agents would fall into the never-ending deadlock loop of hello-sending. However, such is not the case, because once included, `hello` remains in the set of beliefs, so it cannot be included again (unless removed beforehand) and the plan would not become launched again.

Buyers sends the `require(Ware)` belief to Seller, where Ware is a variable containing gas in this case. This plan is conditional and is executed only if there is a requirement for some goods among the agent's beliefs (otherwise the dialogue is over).

Seller checks whether it has the required thing in stock and if so, it executes an `!offer` subplan. This plan adds `offered(buyer,gas)` to Seller's belief set. It means that Seller knows that it offered *gas* to *buyer*. Then the current price of gas is retrieved (line 21, Listing 3.5) and sent to Buyer.

On Buyer's side there are two plans for the evaluation of incoming *price/2* beliefs. The first occurs if the offered price cannot be accepted (is higher than the maximum acceptable price). Then *require/2* at Seller is removed ("untelled" – line 20, Listing 3.4). Otherwise the latter is executed and `buy(Ware)` is sent. In the case of canceling the purchase request, Seller removes the `offered(S,Ware)` belief from its belief set (lines 16–17, Listing 3.5).

One can object that there are no desires and intentions in our example. They are there, but they are handled automatically by the infrastructure. However, in this case, the conduct of the agent is indeed very simple.

BDI architecture certainly has its pros and cons. Among the advantages of BDI is the ability to mimic human behavior and to perform relatively complex reasoning. Moreover, BDI is probably the most widespread approach with many implementations, which makes its use easier, because there is an elaborated theory, development tools, a large body of documentation, a lot of experience and a community of developers and scientists. Many features that need to be manually implemented under other agent approaches are inherent properties of this concept and are instantly ready to use.

On the other hand, BDI architecture is "heavy," which means that there is a substantial system overhead and the system demands a lot of computational power, which can be a problem in the case of "mega-scale" applications with hundreds of thousands or even millions of agents (the requirement can appear in agent-based simulations).[63] BDI agents are relatively complex, and so are multi-agent systems that are composed of them. Hence, many unintended or even unwanted features can easily show up in such systems. Nwana expressed other objections against this agent architecture:

"First, while traditional planning researchers and classical decision theorists question the necessity for having all of these epistemic attitudes (i.e., beliefs, desires, intentions), DAI[64] researchers with a sociological bias question why they only have three! Secondly, the logics underpinning these agents, mostly second-order modal logics, have not been investigated fully and their relevance in practice is questionable."[65]

---

[63]The problem is even worsened by the fact that most existing BDI implementations are based on Java, which consumes another large amount of system resources.
[64]Distributed Artificial Intelligence
[65]Nwana 1996.

Anyway, BDI is a flourishing concept and one of the few fields within the realm of agents that did not remain just a theoretical scientific model, but was able to materialize into a more "tangible" formal theory, languages, frameworks and a lot of practical applications. Thus the question is not whether it is a useful idea or not, but rather for which application it could be convenient.

3.5   Hybrid agents

In the foregoing chapters we have discussed various approaches to the construction of software agents. Each kind of agent has its advantages and disadvantages, and so it is often the best option to combine available alternatives and create the best one out of them. *Hybrid agents* are therefore the kind of agents that are composed of more *layers*, where each layer is built under different agent architecture. Using various agent architectures we can pick the most convenient features of each chosen concept; nevertheless, we must deal, on the other hand, with the problem of their mutual interference.

Every hybrid agent must have indeed at least two layers, where each of them is of a different architecture. The overall behavior of the system depends on the concept of the layers as well as on their alignment. According to Wooldridge,[66] there are three basic types of layering:

- *Horizontal layering* – in horizontally layered architectures, all software layers are connected directly to the sensory input and action output. Each layer works as a distinct agent and generates suggestions for what to do. The advantage of this layering it its simplicity – each layer can be designed separately, without bindings to other layers and putting them together. On the other hand there must be a *mediator*, a system part that is responsible for the distribution of inputs and communication among the layers. Design of such mediator can be relatively difficult, as there are m^n possible interactions and there is a risk of its overloading.

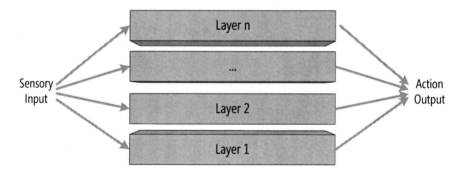

Figure 3.11 – Horizontal layering

- *Vertical layering* – in vertically layered architectures, the input passes through the layers and is handled by more than one layer. The inter-layer interaction is much simpler, as there is a need for communication just between two neighboring layers. On the other hand, the system performance is lower, because all communica-

---

[66]Wooldridge 2002, p. 98.

tion has to pass through the entire system. The error that appears in one layer is spreading through the system.

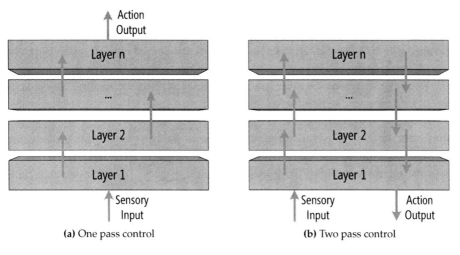

(a) One pass control   **(b)** Two pass control

Figure 3.12 – Vertical layering

- *One pass control* – the input flows through the architecture one way until the last layer makes the final action output. This configuration has a better performance, but there is no feedback among the layers.

- *Two pass control* – the input goes through the architecture the same way as in the one-pass case; however, the result generated by the last layers does not leave the agent but goes back through all the layers. The configuration looks like the organizational hierarchy.[67] It means that for this architecture typically a broadening scope of bottom-up and top-down competence increases the specialization of layers.

The main advantage of this concept is the ability to pick desired features of various agency architectures. Several disadvantages should be taken into consideration as well: there is no hybrid agent architecture (at least so far), so their design is always created ad hoc with the attendant problems; there is no deeply elaborated theory behind them; and they tend to be very application-specific.[68]

---

[67] Ibid., p. 99.
[68] Nwana 1996.

3.6   Chapter summary

Agents exist in environments that determine their aspects. We can divide agent environments according to various traits such as: accessibility, determinism, dynamics, discreetness, episodicness or dimensionality. Agents can be defined as autonomous, decision-making units with diverse characteristics. Agents can perceive their environment, can take actions towards it and towards other agents and can communicate with other agents. The environment can on the other hand take actions towards the agents. Their characteristics include: reactiveness, social abilities, initiative, goal-orientation and autonomy.

There are several approaches to agency. Reactive agents do not create a symbolic representation of their surroundings and behave on the basis of the percepts from the environment instead. The intelligence of the system built on the reactive agents comes from the agent interactions. There are various architectures of reactive agents, including subsumption architecture, dynamic subsumption architecture and agent network architecture. Deliberative agents are a more sophisticated kind of agents that create a symbolic representation of their surroundings in their memories. Among the most important principles of their function are the approach driven by utility, the logic-based approach and the BDI approach. Hybrid agents represent a combination of principles within one agent.

Chapter 4
Agent interactions

So far, we have discussed agents as the individual units, but the power of multi-agent systems stems from agent interactions and inter-operation. The agents pursue their goals not alone, but in relationship with other agents. As the agents encounter, communicate, cooperate or compete mutually, new emergent properties of the system appear. Study of these interactions is an important step to comprehension of the whole field.

As there is no simple definition of an agent, the definition of agent interaction is also tricky. For our purposes we can consider that each agent has its "sphere of influence" as a theoretical area of its interest. The agent interaction occurs where such spheres overlap. Overlapping interests can be either consistent or conflicting. Both cases require a different method of agent conduct in order to pursue a set of goals. In the foregoing chapters, various approaches to agent design were discussed. This chapter is generally about the agent interactions without ties to particular agent principles.

There is a handful of ways to tackle the issue. One of the approaches distinguishes three kinds of agent relationship according to the mode of interaction:

- *Coordination* – reaching goals by obeying common rules

- *Cooperation* – agents work together to reach a common goal

- *Competition* – there is a rivalry between agents for a common goal or resource. This interaction is indeed conflicting.

Game theory offers useful instruments to describe the agent interactions.

Coordination is the simplest principle. The agents have to follow certain norms and rules that are intended to prevent further conflicts. A good example of such system is traffic rules that allow cars (agents) to avoid collisions and keep the whole system of independent entities working. Coordination in this context is a very efficient principle of conflict avoidance, because there is no need for communication, negotiation and other advanced relationships among agents and therefore it is easy to implement. It could be a good choice in static and relatively simple systems with a small state space that do not change through the time; however, it is much less useful in changing and evolving systems, because the rules must be stated beforehand and the system cannot adapt to new conditions easily. In the case of more sophisticated systems, it is often a challenge to cover and set the rules for all its possible states.

Suppose a crossing with right-hand priority and two cars on it (see Figure 4.1). If both will follow the rule – that is, the car on the right will go and the car on the left will wait – the intersection will be cleared safely, which is a desirable outcome. If just one of the participating agents breached the rule, then either a collision (the car on the left did not yield to the right) or a jam (the car on the right did not go) would occur. Both cases are undesirable. The last possibility is that both parties violate the rule (i.e., the car on the right would yield to the left). Strictly from the game theory point of view, the case is desirable, because no accident could occur. Game theory has a model named "Game of chicken" that describes such a situation. In this model, there are two Nash equilibria, that is two situations that the agent can rationally do. Multiple Nash equilibria bring unwanted uncertainty. To remove such uncertainty, we should remove all the redundant Nash equilibria using rules that impose punishments on them, or set the system such that the situation is not even possible.

		Right car	
		Follow	Breach
Left car	Follow	1 / 1	0 / 0
	Breach	−5 / −5	1 / 1

(a) Two cars on the intersection with right hand priority. Without any penalty for breaching the rule, there is no difference if both cars follow the rules or both break it. Two Nash equilibria make the situation risky.

		Right car	
		Follow	Breach
Left car	Follow	1 / 1	0 / 0
	Breach	−5 / −5	−1 / −1

(b) If we impose a penalty for breaching the rules, there is just one Nash equilibrium.

Figure 4.1 – Example of coordination interaction – cars on an intersection

Coordination based on rules creates dependencies among agents. Such dependencies can be sources of complicated relationships. In pure coordination-based systems, where negotiation is not possible to resolve exceptional situations, it could be a source of severe problems like deadlocks.

There can be distinguished the following kinds of dependencies among agents:[1]

- *Independence* – agents are independent of each other

- *Unilateral dependence* – one agent is dependent on the other, but not vice versa

- *Reciprocal dependence* – both agents are dependent on each other, but they do not need to pursue the same goal

- *Mutual dependence* – both agents are dependent on each other with the same goal (this is a special case of the reciprocal dependence).

The last two cases can cause deadlocks and similar states of the system.

Establishing proper rules can avoid the undesirable situations, nonetheless the issue is how the rules can be enforced. Generally, there are two possibilities:

- *Ex ante* – the agent has no choice whether to follow or breach the rule, because the rules are hardcoded in its behaviors. This approach is present in the vast majority of multi-agent systems, thanks to its relative simplicity.

- *Ex post* – the agent has a choice whether to break the rule or not, and if it does, it could be punished. Such an approach is much closer to our everyday experience; however, it is so intricate to implement that it is very rare in multi-agent systems.

Cooperation is the mode of interaction where a shared resource or conflicting goal[2] is present, but the clash cannot be resolved by existing rules. Most such situations can be modeled as cooperative games (a game-theory term), which means that agents can be better off if they resolve the conflict by *negotiation*. Negotiation is the process leading to a negotiated rule that is valid for the particular situation among two (and sometimes more) agents. Such a rule is often called a *contract*. The negotiation process is governed by a set of rules called a *negotiation protocol* that describes all the valid states, options, languages, ontologies and any other parameters of communication. Negotiation is indeed possible only in the situation where the agents can communicate and use a common negotiation protocol.

---

[1]Sichman et al. 1994.

[2]Scarce or shared resources could be, for example, a free capacity of memory or a certain simulated value like budget or working capacity. A conflicting goal is a goal that can be reached by just one competing party (the winner), although multiple agents pursue it.

Protocols can be of various levels of intricacy, from as simple as the exchange of two messages to very sophisticated ones with complicated protocol covering all possible exceptions. Good negotiation protocols should fulfill the following requirements (inspired by Sandholm[3]):

- *Guaranteed ending* – the protocol should guarantee that the negotiation will end with a conclusion in finite time. Negotiation could end with a contract or simply come to the statement that an agreement is not feasible; but the protocol should never fall into a deadlock.

- *Pareto-efficiency* – the resulting contract should maximize total welfare. It refers to a situation where no one can be better off without making the other party worse off. If the contract allowed one agent reaching a higher utility without hurting the other one, it would be obvious that the employed protocol was misleading.

- *Credibility* – the parties have the incentive to bargain according to the rules. It means that the negotiation protocol should make the participants avoid breaking rules or trying to deceive the other party.

- *Neutrality* – the protocol should be neutral, which means it should not influence the behavior of the parties. The negotiation protocol is a formal arrangement and a medium of negotiation, and as such it should be independent of the contents. If the protocol influenced the behavior of the parties, it would mean that it could prevent the agents from behaving optimally.

- *Distribution* – the negotiation protocol should not require any central points if possible. If central points (like communication hubs, etc.) are required, there is a risk of the creation of bottlenecks and hard-pressed loci in the system, which can have adverse effects on performance.

- *Simplicity* – the negotiation protocol should be as simple and fast as possible. This is rather a practical requirement, and very important, because the more complex the protocol, the higher the risk of errors and unintended states it brings.

There can be basic modes of negotiation that differ in the number of participants on both sides and hence in their complexity.

- *One-to-one* – one agent is bargaining with one other. This mode can cover the widest range of problems. The preferences are typically symmetric. In most real cases this kind can be modeled as a cooperation game and therefore the parties have a chance to find a common interest. The bargaining could be theoretically simple, but its actual implementation could be challenging.

---

[3]Sandholm 1999.

The following two modes are *competitive*, because due to their complexity, parties have a lower chance to find an efficient common interest and a cooperative strategy.

- *One-to-many* – one agent is simultaneously negotiating with a number of others. This scenario is typical for resource allocation (e.g., customer-producers; employer-applicants, etc.). Various types of auctions could be particularly efficient in this situation.

- *Many-to-many* – a very complex mode when the negotiations are hard to manage. A good solution could be to establish "a central point" and treat the situation as in a one-to-many mode, or to use some advanced auctioning principle (e.g., the case of stock exchanges). In some cases, the interests of some agents are compatible and they can then create alliances and act as one party.

Competition is the mode of interaction when the agents compete for a scarce resource or conflicting goal, because cooperation is impossible or inefficient. As stated above, in the vast majority of cases of at least one-to-one relationships, cooperation is a preferable means of interaction.

Among the cases when cooperation is not possible are the following:

- *Zero-sum games* are the situations when the gain of one agent is exactly offset by a loss of the other. There is no common interest that could be traded and hence nothing to negotiate. Actually true zero-sum games are very rare, but people often tend to consider situations zero-sum games even if they are cooperative.

  Suppose two agents that have to complete certain task, but they need a common resource that is enough for only one of them. They have four options (see Figure 4.2). The first is that both agents try to complete the task, but they deplete the scarce resource and no one will succeed. In the second case, one agent will try to do the task, the latter will cease. The third option is the same situation with the swapped agents. In both cases, the agent that tries to complete the task will succeed, the other will fail. The last one is the situation when both agents give up and the task indeed will not be completed. If the agents pursue the common goal of the entire system (that is, their objective is to finish the task, no matter who will do it – the so-called benevolence assumption), the situation is clear: the agents negotiate who will complete the task and who will refrain and the task will be done. They have one total utility that is the sum of the utilities of both agents:

$$E(U) = E(U_1) + E(U_2), \tag{4.1}$$

$$E_1(U) = -1 + (-1) = -2, \tag{4.2}$$

$$E_2(U) = -1 + 1 = 0, \tag{4.3}$$

$$E_3(U) = 1 + (-1) = 0, \tag{4.4}$$

$$E_4(U) = -1 + (-1) = -2, \tag{4.5}$$

where $E_x(U)$ is the expected utility for the respective case.

If it does matter which agent finishes the task (i.e., the agents are self-interested), the situation looks purely competitive like a zero-sum game, but it is actually still a cooperation. Without negotiation, the Nash equilibrium of the game is the first case: both try, no one succeeds. With negotiation, they can draw lots, for who will complete the task. Without negotiation and without drawing, both agents surely fail. With negotiation and with drawing, each of them has a 50% chance to fail and 50% chance to complete the task, which is still a better situation than without negotiation.

$$E_{nd}(U_1) = -1; E_{nd}(U_2) = -1, \tag{4.6}$$

$$E_d(U_1) = 0.5(-1) + 0.5(1) = 0; E_d(U_2) = 0.5(1) + 0.5(-1) = 0. \tag{4.7}$$

There is no total utility as the agents are self-interested, but both agents are better off cooperating anyway. This means that cooperation can bring a higher expected utility and so the situation is also cooperative. True zero-sum games are uncommon.

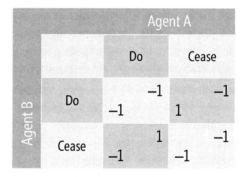

Figure 4.2 – Payoff matrix of the game of two agents competing for a scarce resource. If they agree that they will draw for who will complete the task, they can reach a higher utility than without such an agreement.

- *Cooperative games when negotiation is impossible* are the most common competitive situations. As stated above, negotiation is a necessary assumption for any cooperative interaction. In cases when negotiation is not possible or is inefficient (for example due to a too-high number of participants), competitive interaction takes place. A good example would be an auction. If bidders collude and keep the price of the auctioned object low, they can then divide the profits they earn this way (at the expense of the seller, of course). This is, however, possible only in the case that the number of bidders is low; otherwise the costs of collusion are high due to a complicated negotiation, the need to ensure that all parties will keep the promise, and the low shares of profit divided among many parties. In some situations collusion could be simply forbidden, which is a plausible option in an agent-based simulation, but it is much less feasible in a real-life situation (as through an anti-monopoly policy), because enforcement of such a ban is sometimes tricky.

4.1 Agent communication

For any agent interaction, communication between agents is necessary. Communication between agents typically happens via sending messages between them, just as in the case of objects (where messaging is performed by calling object methods). However, agent messaging is more sophisticated.

The agents actually typically do not communicate directly, but they send a message to a messaging subsystem of their agent environment and the messaging subsystem delivers the message to the recipient. The messaging subsystem could be somehow similar to e-mail service. It should be able to cope with situations like a nonexistent recipient, rejection (agents have free will), and so on. Messages can be sent to more recipients at once.

The medium of communication is a communication language. There is a whole body of work devoted to agent communication languages. Some authors consider the existence of general agent communication language an important part of the whole agent paradigm.[4] In accordance with this view, various languages are used.

KIF[5] (stands for Knowledge Interchange Format) defines a content of the message using logical statements. It is based on first-order logic. It works with variables, functions, Boolean connectives, quantifiers and other logical apparatus. Of course, some ontology to construct such message is needed. KIF is not originally an agent language, but an attempt at a general language for passing knowledge.

Listing 4.1 – The example of KIF message. The wage of agent1 is $10. (KIF)

```
(= (wage agent1) (scalar 10 Dollar)
```

Languages like _KQML_[6] (Knowledge Query and Manipulation Language) or _FIPA ACL_[7] define the character of a message, with its envelope containing how and to whom the message should be delivered, but not its contents. Contents of the message could be in KIF, Prolog, Lisp or any other language.

---

[4]Shoham 1993.
[5]Genesereth 1991.
[6]Finin, McKay, and Fritzson 1992.
[7]_FIPA ACL Message Structure Specification_ 2002.

Listing 4.2 – The example of KQML containing KIF message sent to `firm2` agent using `MONEY` ontology. (KQML)

```
(ask-one
    :content  ((=(wage  A1)  (scalar  10  Dollar))
    :receiver  firm2
    :language  KIF
    :ontology  MONEY
)
```

Languages like KIF or KQML are universal, but their important disadvantage is their "weight." Proper construction, validation and comprehension of messages are extremely demanding and resource-consuming. Thanks to their robustness, they are suitable for artificial-intelligence applications and other implementation with a lower number of relatively sophisticated agents. For the same reason, they are seldom used for agent-based simulations, especially for those with a higher number of agents, where the performance of the system is an issue. For agent-based simulations, specific single-purpose languages and protocols (e.g., consisting just of simple keywords and values) are often used. Inter-agent messaging is then generic as in the case of objects.

4.2 Chapter summary

Perhaps the most important part of multi-agents systems is not the agents alone, but their interactions, because agents' relations create the emergent properties of the system. Agent interactions can be divided according to various criteria. In this book we have used the following categories: coordination (reaching goals by obeying common rules), cooperation (agents work together to reach a common goal) and competition (if there is a rivalry between agents for a common goal or resource). For cooperation, negotiation is an important process. It is performed on the basis of negotiation protocol that should follow certain principles. They are: guaranteed ending, pareto-efficiency, credibility, neutrality, distribution and simplicity. In competitive situations, parties struggle for a scarce resource. Zero-sum games occur when there is no space for negotiation or when a cooperative solution is infeasible (when the negotiation is for instance impossible).

For any agent relationship, communication among agents is necessary. Various languages were developed for that purpose.

Chapter 5
Agent-oriented programming

So far we have discussed the multi-agent systems as more or less a theoretical concept. In the moment we want to develop tangible multi-agent systems, particularly agent-based simulations, we need a concrete approach for how to do it. In the general field of information systems development, several engineering methodologies have emerged. Over the last 25 years, object-oriented programming and object-oriented design have become a predominant paradigm and most of the information systems are developed this way. Although there is no generally accepted model of object-oriented programming, it has become a kind of *de facto* standard allowing a boom of object-oriented programming languages and frameworks for their easy use and training.

Unlike attempts to standardize agent communication, interactions, abstract system architecture and other inter-agent matters, there is much less done on the adoption of concepts of the mere agents. There is a wide variety of definitions of architecture and principles of software agent development that are mutually incompatible. Authors often build their own definitions for the purposes of their particular subfields of interest. Almost each article about agents the author has read, and each agent methodology the author has studied, treats agents differently. "Agent" is actually a very vague term. Without agreement on the principles of an agent-oriented paradigm, truly agent-oriented languages can hardly be developed and supported.

Perhaps the most cited work relating to this topic is Shoham's article on agent-oriented programming.[1] Shoham considers agent-oriented programming a special case of object-oriented programming. Unlike the object-oriented approach, where the internal state of the object is generic, agents, according to Shoham, consist of components like beliefs, decisions, capabilities and obligations that constitute a *mental state* of the agent that is described formally in an extension of standard epistemic logic. Coding of messages is not application-specific, but a common *agent communication language* is used. In fact, Shoham's work does not offer a general programming paradigm on a conceptual level like object-oriented programming, but rather a particular logic-based agency approach.

---

[1]Shoham 1993.

Biswas[2] considers agent classes the patterns of agent instantiation. They are defined as 10-tuples consisting of such characteristics as information attributes, mental components, domain classes, knowledge base, communication languages, ontologies, interaction protocols, methods for communication, methods for migration and intelligent methods for knowledge acquisition. Agents deal with three types of abstractions: generalization, association and cooperation.

The aforementioned papers consider agents a part of the artificial intelligence "realm," which the author deems impractical. Multi-agent systems have grown from artificial intelligence roots, but nowadays they represent a separate technology. Hence the need for a general, independent concept of artificial intelligence.

Van Dyke Parunak et al.[3] propose another approach. They treat agents from a software engineering perspective and instead of a mentalistic, artificial-intelligence-based approach they focus on the representation of agents and their roles in the social system. Their concept is an extension of UML for the representation of multi-agent systems. The same idea was used by the AUML initiative in their effort to develop the Agent UML specification.[4] This approach is more useful for practical implementation than the approach based on agent mental states, because it treats agents more as software entities than logical constructs. However, the author does not consider it a proper approach. Agents are an independent concept. Attempts to graft them onto existing object-oriented methodologies could lead to confusing results. On one hand it is convenient to capitalize on existing and widespread standards; on the other hand, any abstract model should lead to an easier contemplation of the underlying issue. This may not occur if the method used is too complicated, which can occur in this case.

Gomez-Sanz et al.[5] state that there is still no consensus on an agent software engineering paradigm, which is considered a serious hurdle for the development of the whole field.

5.1   Principles of software agents

A software agent is a software entity resembling an object or software component Unlike objects, agents have a time dimension. This means that objects actually do something only at times when some of their methods are called, and otherwise they stay inactive as a data structure in operating memory. They are naturally synchronous. If some sort of parallelism or asynchronous behavior is needed, it has to be implemented explicitly. Agents, on the other hand, exist in parallel and work asynchronously by their nature (they work continually, not just in the discrete moments of time – hence the time dimen-

---

[2]Biswas 2008.
[3]Parunak and Odell 2001.
[4]*FIPA Modeling: Agent Class Diagrams* 2003; *FIPA Modeling: Interaction Diagrams* 2003.
[5]Gomez-Sanz et al. 2008.

sion) due to their principle of autonomy. As mentioned above, autonomy means the control over actions and internal states. It is feasible only when the entity can control its operation independently at any moment of its life. If an agent should wait until an external factor passes control to it, it cannot be called truly autonomous (it indeed depends on the particular implementation, how this feature is accomplished).

Autonomy is provided by the agent's operations that we call *behaviors*. As methods are the means of operation of objects, behaviors are the means of operation of agents. The main difference between method and behavior is that while a method is of a one-shot nature and is unparallel and synchronous by default, a behavior runs in time and is parallel and asynchronous (although there can be one-shot behaviors as well). It actually means that if we need to implement some continuous action in an object-oriented world, we need to code a cycle into the method that performs a kind of action cyclically. In an agent-oriented world, this is implicit. Behaviors communicate using messages that are indeed typically asynchronous as well. Using messages, they pass information and parameters. Unlike objects, they do not pass control this way (as they are asynchronous by default).

Autonomy also implies that an agent has exclusive access to its *data*. If any external entity had a chance to manipulate directly with the agent's data, the agent would not be able to have control over them, and that could prevent it from pursuing its goals.

In object-oriented programming, there is essentially just one kind of message passing: calling of method.[6] Thanks to their social abilities and reactiveness, agents step into the interactions with other agents and with the environment that surrounds them. An environment of software agents is a computer system that allows operation of agents and provides necessary services for their execution (creation, disposal, messaging, name services, and the like). In agent-oriented programming we can distinguish three basic kinds of interactions: communication, perception and action.

- *Communication* – a temporary interaction between two or more agents. It is voluntary for both sides. No agent is obliged to step into such a relationship; each side can cancel the communication at any time (the concrete situation depends on the negotiation protocol); and the agent is not obliged to reply to sent messages. There is no direct counterpart to agent communication in the object-oriented realm. Unlike objects, for agents, communication is an inherent feature. Communication is an exhibition of the agent's social abilities.

- *Percepts* are information from the environment that represent an agent's sensory input. For an agent it is voluntary information – it is not obliged to react or even receive it, but the environment has to provide the information. In the real world,

---

[6]Of course, we can mention also the case when a value is put directly into object attribute with public scope, but it is not a "clean" way of message passing.

perception would provide the kind of information that is objectively recogniz-
able (e.g., temperature). There is no direct counterpart to percepts in the object-
oriented world. Perception is an exhibition of an agent's reactiveness.

- *Action* (or action call) is a one-way and one-shot relationship when one agent willingly influences its agent environment or another agent, or the environment influences an agent. Unlike the aforementioned relationships, it is voluntary just for
one side – the originator of the relation – but it is obligatory for the other side.
Actions in the agent world resemble natural laws in the real world. We have no
option other than to obey gravity, for example. In the software world, there are no
such strict, natural rules, but rules are sometimes needed (for instance, the mere
creation of the agent cannot be its voluntary act). Hence rules must be hardwired
into the code. A counterpart of actions in object-oriented programming is method-
calling, because the object whose method is called also has no choice whether to
execute it or not. As mentioned above, an action could be performed between
agents or between agent and environment. An agent's action call of another agent
is – according to the author's experience – relatively rare, and this type of relationships is often of a negative nature (e.g. disposing of other agents), but it may not
be always true. Anything the agent does, for example movement, is its action applied to the environment. Actions of the environment imposed on agents (creation
of agents or changes of parameters) are typically more common than the actions
among agents. Action, like perception, is an exhibition of an agent's reactiveness.

The model of agent interaction is depicted in Figure 3.1 on page 25.

Objects encapsulate program and data together in order to insure proper handling
of data according to the required rules. Objects, however, still remain mere instruments
without any inherent purpose and so they will interact with data in any correct way. In
other words, they can be used to pursue the goal of the system as a whole. Agents go
further and add *goals* and interests to the code and data. An agent still has the ability
to interact with its data in a proper way, but in addition it may do so in order to reach
objectives that it was designed for. Unlike objects that are entirely passive and will do
what they are asked to do, agents are active administrators of their data and will do what
is needed no matter whether they are asked or not; and on the other hand, they could
reject requests that would be against their goals.

Initiative and goal-orientation are also important agent characteristics. Initiative is
the ability to initiate actions independently, without external stimuli. An agent's initiative depends on its goal-orientation. An agent cannot take initiative without a goal that
would drive their conduct. If we have no goals, we can just react to incoming information, but we cannot perform our own action, because we have no reason why we should
do it, lacking objectives that we should pursue.

Goal-orientation is a key distinguishing aspect of agents compared to objects. For the aforementioned reasons, the author considers agents a next-order abstraction after objects, in the same manner as object-orientation is a next-order abstraction in relation to the structured approach. In the course of time, the concepts of software development evolve towards a greater encapsulation and localization.[7] Programs of the first computers were monolithic. There was at best a primitive modularization; the whole program and all its structures were one piece of code. Structured programming has brought the segmentation of code into separate modules: functions, procedures, and so on. Object-oriented programming has bound them up with their data. Agent-oriented programming adds goals that are tied to code and data.[8] See Table 5.1 for a comparison of software paradigms.

Table 5.1 – Evolution of software paradigms. Inspired by Odell 2003

	Monolithic Programming	Structured Programming	Object-oriented Programming	Agent-oriented Programming
Modularity	Nonmodular	Modular	Modular	Modular
Data	External	External	Internal	Internal
Unit Invocation	External	External	External	Internal

It is important to mention that there are other interpretations as well. Some authors consider agent-oriented programming a special case of object-oriented programming with certain specific traits.[9] This is indeed possible, but such a view narrows an agent's application domain to certain particular purposes. Moreover, objects are more a special case of agents than vice versa, as an object possesses a subset of an agent's features (it can be considered an agent with one-shot behaviors – see below – and the action mode of interaction only). Therefore the understanding of agents as the descendants of objects sounds more convenient.

What can goal-oriented software be good for? First, contemporary applications often contain some aspects of artificial intelligence, automated decision-making and other advanced functionalities. Employing goal-oriented autonomous agents could be convenient for certain kinds of applications, because they could provide desired intelligent behavior. Second, goal-orientation can be useful in complex, distributed systems composed of many single units, as is typical for grid computing. Particularly, coordination of such systems can be sometimes troublesome due to certain spontaneous effects that can emerge, such as bottlenecks or deadlocks. Complicated algorithms and procedures on the macro level of the whole system are often used to solve such problems. Goal-oriented

---

[7]Odell 2003.

[8]Note that each step in this evolution allowed developing much more sophisticated code with much less effort and knowledge what has ultimately led to ever falling prices of software.

[9]Shoham 1993.

units on the micro level can provide an easier solution, as they can be developed not only to perform the required calculation, but also be equipped with the goal to deliver the results as needed. Third, the goal-oriented approach can be a fruitful mindset to software development. Unlike the traditional procedural concept of programming, where we are focused on an algorithm, orientation toward objectives is close to the declaratory approach, where the keystone of a solution is the definition of required results. Finally, there are many other particular applications in various subfields of multi-agent systems where this feature could be exploited. In agent-based simulations (our primary subject of interest), for instance, there is a need for self-directed and goal-oriented entities that represent economic agents in order to simulate economic reality. A clash of their interests in the simulated environment can allow studying the behavior of people in various situations.

5.2   Agents as software entities

We have discussed the general characteristics of software agents. How should an agent actually be represented? Because we consider the agent-oriented paradigm a descendant of the object-oriented approach, it conveniently could use many principles introduced with object-oriented programming, particularly: *instantiation*, *inheritance* and *encapsulation*.

Agent classes (sometimes cited as agent types[10]) are widely accepted as patterns for agent instances in exactly the same way as object classes are patterns for object instances in object-oriented programming. For example, suppose a Person agent class defining the structure of Person agents. Numerous agent-instances with various names and other properties can be derived from the Person class. Once an agent (instance) is created according to the "recipe" in the agent class, its behaviors start to operate, communicate, accept percepts and perform actions.

Agent classes can be designed as children of existing classes and inherit their features. Although inheritance does not directly result from agent characteristics, there are practical reasons for agent platforms to support it. The child agents would have all behaviors of the parent; they can add new properties and overlay the existing ones. There can be various kinds of inheritance (one ancestor vs. multiple ancestors, etc.), depending on the particular platform.

Polymorphism is often deemed one of the most powerful features of object-oriented programming. In the world of agents, polymorphism in its traditional meaning is superfluous, as an agent's messages are generic and the communication between agents of any class is possible naturally.

---

[10]Wagner 2003.

Encapsulation in the object realm means the union of code and data. In terms of its agent-oriented meaning, encapsulation includes code represented by an agent's *behaviors*, *data* in the agent's data stores and *goals*.

5.2.1 Behaviors

As mentioned above, an agent's conduct is carried out entirely by the agent's behaviors, which react to incoming stimuli, adjust internal data structures and perform the agent's actions. Each agent can have multiple behaviors. Each behavior is executed continually, unless it is declared one-shot. In every run, it checks if conditions have changed (because of new messages, percepts, changes in data or changes in goals) and behaves accordingly (by sending messages, performing actions, changing data stores or adjusting goals). There must be at least the behaviors for handling all possible action calls. Some behaviors can be declared one-shot and then they are performed just once. A typical example is *constructor* and *destructor* behaviors that can be introduced as the counterparts to constructor and destructor methods from object-oriented languages. Constructor is a special behavior that is called after the creation of the agent and its purpose is to set it up. Destructor is another special kind of behavior that is called just before disposing of the agent, and its goal is indeed to tear it down correctly.

5.2.2 Data

Besides behaviors as a means of agent operations, an agent could have memory to keep its internal state (analogous to an object's attributes). Actually this could be anything from a primitive variable, an object, set of logical facts, database or any other kind of data store. It could be physically a separate entity or a special object within the agent. An agent's behaviors should have an exclusive access (at least theoretically) to its data due to the principle of autonomy. On the other hand, public access to the agent's data should be also technically available on a particular agent platform for practical reasons. In object-oriented languages, direct access to the data of particular instance is deemed a bad practice; however, it is also mostly supported.

5.2.3 Goals

Even though agent goals should be specified in the design phase, it is tricky to include them as a peculiar item, especially if we strive to develop an abstract, conceptually independent model. Therefore, in most cases, the goals would be typically embedded merely in the code of agent's behaviors and in the manner of agent's reasoning.[11] In more so-

---

[11]Some agent languages – for example, AgentSpeak(L) – allow explicit goal specification (see section 3.4.3). However, it is practical for some cases of logic based agent approaches. In some other cases it could be troublesome.

phisticated systems, the goals need not even be determinate; rather they can be changing through the time and therefore they can be stored in certain data structure in symbolic form. Anyway, unlike objects, agents always somehow contain goals.

5.3 Agent features

All agent features discussed so far are conceptual. Every implementation must adapt them for the needs of the specific platform. For instance, if we were developing reactive agents (see chapter 3.3), they would have no explicit goals hardwired anyway and their objectives would stem organically from their emergent patterns of conduct and parameters of the environment where they are present. In that case they would have no data, their behaviors would respect certain particular architecture and their goals would be embodied in the structure of their behaviors. If we were developing a BDI agent, it would be equipped with behaviors for handling beliefs, desires, intentions, plans and the respective data stores.

To sum up, an agent platform should allow the implementation of the following conceptual functionalities. Some of these are mandatory due to the agent characteristics and each agent platform should implement them; some are optional and may not be offered by some platforms.

1 Agents are instantiated from agent classes (inheritance and abstract agent classes can be supported).

2 Agents contain behaviors as the means of operation. The environment should allow their continuous and parallel execution. Special one-shot behaviors that are executed as non-recurring as well as constructor and destructor behaviors can be implemented.

3 Agents contain data stores where their data (internal state) are kept. Private access to the data must be guaranteed for the agent. Optionally other modes of access can be available for practical purposes.

4 The framework should allow three kinds of interactions: generic communication, action calls and perception. Each agent must contain behaviors for handling all possible action calls that it can receive. An agent can have behaviors for handling messages and perception. Agent interaction is typically asynchronous.

5 Agent platforms can offer special instruments for implementing goals. Otherwise, goals are incorporated into behaviors.

One can argue that there is not so sharp a distinction between agents (according to the above rules) and objects. However, there are the intrinsic differences between objects and software agents that make agents an independent principle. The author would mention at least the following:

First, objects support just one kind of messaging – the method call, with parameters of defined structure. "Reception" of message is obligatory and typically synchronous. Agents, on the contrary, support multiple modes of communication. Besides receiving and calling actions that resemble object method calls, there is also direct messaging and perception that are voluntary for the agent. Second, agent's behaviors work asynchronously and perpetually, unlike object methods. They typically do not pass control. And finally, an agent's conduct is goal-oriented. It can decline performing the requested action if it is against its objectives (except the behavior claimed by the action call).

5.4   Chapter summary

Although principles of multi-agent systems have existed for more than two decades, there is still little consensus on the definition of a mere agent-oriented paradigm, what the software agents look like and what are their standard features. There are many different competing technologies, but a unifying conception is missing, although it would be beneficial for practical use of agent technologies. Open questions include how agents should work, how they should be treated as software entities, and what relationship they have to objects.

Agents can be defined by the following characteristics: autonomy, initiative, reactiveness, goal orientation and social abilities. Autonomy stands for the agent's ability to have control over its action and internal state. It is performed by behaviors that are the means of the agent's operation. The agent has full control over its behaviors and data and will perform solely those actions that comply with its goals. The exhibition of an agent's social abilities and reactiveness are its interaction functionalities, namely: communication among agents, the agent's actions and actions of the environment affecting the agent and the agent's perception. An agent is not obliged to react to communication and to perform perception; however, it must contain behaviors that react to incoming action calls (just as objects react to method calls).

Initiative is the ability to initiate action independently and it is backed by an agent's goal-orientation, which the author considers a key characteristic and the main distinguishing factor between agents and objects. Goals are mostly embedded in behaviors or stored in an agent's data in a certain symbolic way.

Agent-oriented programming is considered a next-order abstraction to object-oriented programming and shares with it certain features, particularly instantiation, inheritance and encapsulation. Agents are instantiated from agent classes. Agent classes can inherit properties from an agent's ancestors. Agents encapsulate code and data as the objects and add goals that provide their purpose-driven conduct.

Chapter 6
Agent-oriented methodologies

The complexity of contemporary information systems, development tools and software development processes brought the need for refining engineering principles, standards and best practices to this field. Today, almost any software development project is managed under a certain methodology (such as RUP, AUP or many others).

The same need is present in the domain of multi-agent systems and especially agent-based simulations. There are enough software frameworks and tools for the development of multi-agent systems, but the methodologies that should guide the users in the design and development process are still weakly established. This is probably mainly due to the fact that a lot of agent frameworks, tools and even the mere simulations are developed as a research initiative at universities and research institutions which feel much less need for standardized development processes and engineered principles. The same fact, on the other hand, constitutes a hurdle for a wider expansion of the simulations based on multi-agent systems.

In the following chapter, a summary of available agent methodologies will be provided, the methodologies will be briefly described and evaluated, and the present situation in the field of multi-agent methodologies will be assessed. The following agent methodologies will be presented:

- Agent Oriented Methodology for Enterprise Modeling
- AUML
- Cassiopeia
- CoMoMAS
- Gaia
- HIM
- MaSE
- MASim
- Prometheus
- Tropos

6.1 Agent Oriented Methodology for Enterprise Modeling

The methodology is focused on building computer manufacturing systems (for manufacturing enterprises) using agent approach. The methodology is based upon object-oriented techniques, especially on the use-case approach.[1]

6.2 AUML

AUML (or Agent UML[2]) is an attempt to extend Unified Modeling Language for the purposes of multi-agent systems. It treats agent programming as the extension and a next abstraction level above object-oriented programming. AUML is backed by the FIPA Modeling Technical Committee. It was established as an ambitious, robust and ample project with a goal to develop (according to their Web site) *"vendor-neutral common semantics, meta-model, and abstract syntax for agent-based methodologies"*. Unfortunately, there has been no development in recent years. The authors of the project note that the project was frozen because UML 2.1 contains certain agent-oriented features, OMG's SysML was released containing some AUML capabilities as well, and The OMG UML Metamodel and Profile for Services (UPMS) RFP was released, which should also include agent-related concepts. However, the project should not be – according to the authors – abandoned finally.

Analogous to UML, AUML is not primarily a methodology that would say what to do, but it is a language that strives to offer tools for using other methodologies. Given that the approach is general and not focused particularly on agent-based simulations, it is not entirely useful for this purpose (for reasons which will be discussed further). Nevertheless, because of its robustness and universal concept it is worth a deeper evaluation.

As mentioned above, the project stems from UML, but is not just its simple extension. The authors of AUML define their interrelationship as follows:

> "Instead of reliance on the OMG's UML, we intend to reuse of UML wherever it makes sense. We do not want to be restricted by UML; we only want to capitalize on it where we can. The general philosophy, then, is: When it makes sense to reuse portions of UML, then do it; when it doesn't make sense to use UML, use something else or create something new."[3]

AUML defines the following types of diagrams:

---

[1] Kendall, Malkoun, and Jiang 1996.
[2] See http://www.auml.org (visited on 9.6.2010)
[3] See http://www.auml.org/auml/main.shtml (visited on 24. 11. 2009)

- Agent Class Diagram

- Sequence Diagram

- Interaction Overview Diagram

- Communication diagram

- Time Diagram

Besides these, there is an Agent Class Diagram Superstructure Meta-model in the methodology that deals with the arrangement of the whole multi-agent system and the organization of agents within it, their interactions and the interoperability of agents from different frameworks.

6.2.1 Agent Class Diagram

Agent Class Diagram stems from the traditional Object Class Diagram and depicts the structure and capabilities of the agent. Each agent has three basic characteristics: identifier, role and organization. Roles define the behavior of an agent in the society, for instance, Seller or Buyer. Agents can have multiple roles in the multi-agent system or they can change from role to role during the execution. Organizations – according to the authors of the standard – define the agent roles and the relationships between these roles. Organizations adhere generally to human or animal organizations such as hierarchies, markets, groups of interest or herds.[4] There can be another optional compartment bearing the information about communication protocol.

Besides the basic properties mentioned above, the agent class has also some other attributes like Capabilities, Services, Language, Ontologies, Knowledge, BDI modalities, Goals, Events, Mobility and Persistence. Just the first two are elaborated in the standard; the rest are still not defined.

Capabilities describe what an agent is able to do and under what conditions.[5] They are represented as an associated class in notation which contains the following compartments: name of the capability, its input and output, input and output constraints and input-output constraints of the capability.

Services are denoted by associated classes as well and they describe services that the agent is able to provide. The attributes of service description are name, description, type of service, interaction protocols supported by the service, agent communication languages, ontology, content language and properties.[6]

---

[4]*FIPA Modeling: Agent Class Diagrams* 2003, p. 3.
[5]Ibid., p. 4.
[6]Ibid., p. 5.

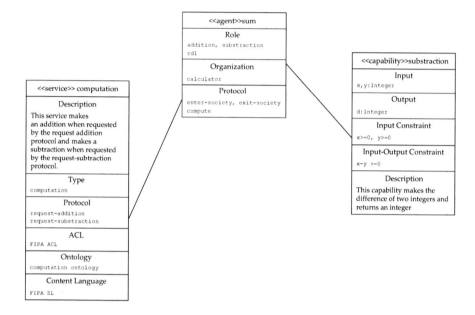

Figure 6.1 – An example of AUML Class Diagram – agent "sum" has one capability (substraction) and one service (computation); Source: *FIPA Modeling: Agent Class Diagrams* 2003, pp. 5–6

6.2.2 Interaction Diagrams

Interaction Diagrams is a group of diagrams in AUML with the purpose to pin down the interaction among agents. They mainly include the improved versions of its object-oriented counterparts. The most important diagram from this group is the Sequence Diagram from UML, which was extended with some agent-oriented features.

The AUML Sequence Diagram provides tools for the description of concurrent communication acts. A message from one agent can be sent in parallel to more recipients. With AUML it is possible to depict the situation when the message is sent to one or more receivers, zero or more receivers or as the exclusive choice when the message is sent to just one of the set of recipients. Sending messages can be influenced by constraints such as time constraints (time frames for finishing communication).

For more advanced communication, protocols can be used. The standard defines various protocols for requests, queries, conditional requests, closing contracts, English auctions, subscriptions, and so on.

Interaction Overview Diagram is a modification of Activity Diagram from UML and depicts the interaction among agents in the control flow of the system. Interaction

Overview Diagrams focus on the overview of the flow of control where the nodes are Interactions or Interaction Occurrences (states).[7]

Communication Diagram models the interactions between agents and sequencing of messages. The information it bears is much the same as the information provided by the Sequence Diagram.

Time Diagram focuses on times of the occurrence of events. Timing diagrams show change in state or other conditions of a structural element over time.[8]

6.2.3 UML 2.1

As was discussed above, the work on AUML was interrupted due to (among other reasons) the release of UML 2.1 which supports agent-oriented features. The approach will be briefly presented in the following discussion based on the article of Dillon et al.[9]

Instead of using Agent Class Diagram, Dillon et al. uses Composite Structure Diagram in order to depict agent structure, especially for the purposes of capturing its goal-driven abilities. The diagram is definitely simpler;[10] however, its ability to capture all the desired information without further textual description is questionable. The interaction among agents is described with the standard Sequence diagram in UML 2.1. Any agent can have more *ports* in order to depict its various roles. As the agent can play multiple roles concurrently, the parallel communication can be depicted in this way.[11]

The author of this book thinks that the problem of AUML is that it is too complex and complicated. It bears a heavy burden of its object-oriented roots. It contains much more features than needed for agent-based simulations and it lacks some other features that are specific for this application domain (e.g., tools for modeling of agent environments). As the language has the ability to encompass and describe all kinds of agents and multi-agent systems, it becomes "heavy" and hard to learn and use. Although the methodology is universal, the BDI approach to agency is promoted in several places. Moreover, the problem of the standard is that it is unfinished and its future development is uncertain.

UML 2.1 seems to be more favorable for the description of agents and multi-agent systems, because it is a standard and it is less complicated than AUML. On the other hand, the question is whether it is the best way to use the existing object-oriented method, trying to adjust it for the purposes of agency.

---

[7]*FIPA Modeling: Interaction Diagrams* 2003, pp. 36–37.
[8]Ibid., p. 39.
[9]Dillon, Dillon, and Chang 2008.
[10]Ibid., p. 7.
[11]Ibid., p. 4.

6.3   Cassiopeia

Cassiopeia is a general methodology for designing multi-agent systems. It is primarily a way to address a type of problem-solving where collective behaviors are put into operation through a set of agents. A multi-agent system should be designed in terms of agents provided with three levels of behavior: elementary, relational and organizational.[12]

The analysis consists of the following steps:

- *Elementary behaviors* – listing of the elementary behaviors that are required for the achievement of a collective task

- *Relational behaviors* – consists of analyzing the organization structure based on the dependencies between the elementary behaviors. These dependencies define the *coupling graph* underlying the collective task being considered. A coupling graph depicts the possible behaviors and their interdependencies. From the dependencies explored this way, the dependencies among agents (called *influences*) are derived and depicted in an *influence graph*.[13]

- *Organizational behaviors* – addresses the dynamics of the organization. It consists in specifying the behaviors that will enable the agents to manage the formation, durability and dissolution of groups.[14]

The methodology is primarily focused on behaviors and relationships among agents. It omits the agent environment. It is interesting but not very suitable for agent-based models.

6.4   CoMoMAS

CoMoMAS[15] is a methodology and environment for the development of multi-agent systems. It is based on CommonKADS[16] methodology, which is focused on knowledge engineering. It is apparent that the methodology is very knowledge-oriented.

The methodology describes the system from five views: the functional view, the competence view, the requirement view, the cooperative view and the social view. Each view corresponds with one type of analysis, which should be done in the following steps.

- *Requirement analysis* – when the requirements are gathered, their interdependencies are identified and the requirements are ranked. *Design model* is the result of this phase.

---

[12]Collinot, Drogoul, and Benhamou 1996.
[13]Ibid., pp. 6–7.
[14]Ibid., p. 7.
[15]Glaser 1997.
[16]Schreiber et al. 1994.

- *Functional analysis* – when the tasks that multi-agent system has to solve are identified, goals, data and control flow are identified. *Task model* is the result of this phase.

- *Competence analysis* – when the problem-solving methods, strategies and behaviors of the agents are determined. *Expertise model* is the result of this phase.

- *Social analysis* – when the relationships among agents are identified, roles, intentions, desires and beliefs of the agents are determined. *System model* is the result of this phase.

- *Cooperative analysis* – when the communication protocols, methods and conflict resolution among the agents are analyzed. *Cooperative model* is the result of this phase.

Finally, the foregoing steps are integrated into the overall agent model and system model describing the organization and the architecture of the multi-agent system.[17]

The methodology contains also the description of knowledge-storing abilities of the agent.

CoMoMAS is definitely a very interesting methodology. It is logical and straightforward. Unfortunately, due to its focus on knowledge it is not very suitable for the purposes of social simulations, as the behavior of agents and not the knowledge is important for this purpose. Nevertheless, there are several interesting ideas in the methodology that can be utilized in our further analysis.

6.5 Gaia

Gaia[18] belongs to the most often cited multi-agent methodologies. It is the universal methodology. The process of the method is divided into three stages: requirements statements, when the requirements are gathered, analysis phase and a design phase.

Analysis is a conceptual phase of the methodology. Its aim is to understand the system and its structure. In the analysis stage of Gaia, there are the following steps:

- Identifying roles in the system. Roles mean individuals, departments or the whole organizations that are included in the system. The result of this phase is the *roles model* – the list of key roles in the system.

- For each role, the associated protocols are documented. Protocols are the patterns of interaction that occur in the system between the various roles. For example, a protocol may correspond to an agent in the role of buyer submitting a bid to

---

[17]Glaser 1997, p. 9.
[18]Wooldridge, Jennings, and Kinny 2000.

another agent in the role of seller. The result of this phase is an interaction model, which captures the recurring patterns of inter-role interaction.[19]

- On the basis of a protocol model, the roles in the system are elaborated. The result is a fully elaborated roles model, which documents the key roles occurring in the system, and their permissions and responsibilities, together with the protocols and activities in which they participate.[20]

All the foregoing steps are iterated until the analysis models are finished.

Design stage is the phase when conceptual analytic models are transformed into lower-level design models that can be used as a basis for a further implementation. The process of the design phase is as follows:

- *Agent model* is created. Agent model describes the individual agent types (i.e., "agent classes"), where each agent type is considered a set of agent roles that were identified in the roles model and agent instances. Agent instances are the specific occurrences of agent type.

- *Service model* should be specified. Services are the individual abilities of the agent. We can compare them with methods in object-oriented programming. Each service can have its inputs, outputs, pre-conditions and post-conditions.

- Finally, the *Acquaintance model* should be developed. Its purpose is to identify the communication paths between the agents in order to discover possible communication bottlenecks.

The author of this book deems Gaia belonging to the best elaborated methodologies. The process focuses on both macro and micro level of the multi-agent system. It is logical and is divided into conceptual and design (i.e., platform-specific) phases. It helps in distinguishing conceptual aspects of the system with those features that are required by the specific implementation and infrastructure used. On the other hand, the methodology is closed and static, which means that it hardly deals with unusual requirements. The methodology does not deal with designing the environment and it is not specifically focused on design of agent-based simulations.

6.6   HIM

High-level and Intermediate Models[21] is a general-purpose multi-agent methodology. It offers five models: a high-level model, an internal agent model for the internal structure of agents, a relationship model, a conversational model and a contract model that captures commitments. The methodology is relatively less known.

---

[19]Wooldridge, Jennings, and Kinny 2000, p. 11.
[20]Ibid., p. 11.
[21]Elammari and Lalonde 1999.

6.7 MaSE

MaSE[22] is a multi-agent methodology focused mainly on robotics. The process of the methodology begins with capturing goals and continues through the conceptual phase to the design of the system. For the support of the methodology an *agentTool* development environment is available.

6.8 MASim

MASim[23] is the only methodology that is focused particularly on agent-based simulations. Due to that fact it is worthy of closer exploration. MASim should cover mainly larger simulations, but it can be used to design and develop smaller ones as well.

The process is divided into five phases:

- The *requirements phase*, which consist of identifying the scope of the simulation model as well as the needs of the application for handling such a model. The requirements are gathered as scenarios from end-users and domain experts of the system (see below). Scenarios are of four types – exogenous that represent external events, influences on the system, endogenous that encompass macro-micro, micro-macro, and peer-peer interactions.

- The *modeling phase*, which aims to construct an abstract model of the system presenting its elements and the dependences between themselves and the system as a whole. In this phase, three steps are performed: resource modeling, when roles and actors are identified; dependency modeling, when dependencies between roles are modeled; and interaction modeling, when the set of interaction protocols is defined.

- The *architectural and design phase*, which translate the model into a set of concrete specifications able to be easily implemented. This phase also intends to identify patterns to be reused in other simulations of the same domain. This is the phase when the conceptual model from the foregoing steps is transformed into a platform-dependent model that will be implemented further.

- The *implementation phase*, where the specifications are coded in programming language.

- The *verification, validation and accreditation* phase, which confronts the overall simulation results with the real system and determines if the simulation application is suitable for the initially required purposes.[24]

---

[22]DeLoach, Wood, and Sparkman 2001.
[23]Campos et al. 2004.
[24]Ibid., p. 4.

The design and development process is cyclical; that is, the individual phases can be repeated if findings in a later phase require adjustments in the previous phase.

The authors of MASim claim the inspiration came from RUP methodology, and unlike many other multi-agent technologies, MASim defines roles involved in the design and development process. The following roles are defined in MASim:

- *End-user*, an individual (or organization) for whom the simulation application is developed. The end-users are responsible for setting up the requirements for the application. They should target the objective of the simulation and define what they expect from the simulation as results.

- *Domain expert*, one or more individuals with deep knowledge about the domain being simulated

- *Modeler*, who along with the end-user and the domain expert are responsible for the construction of the simulation model

- *Software architect*, who is responsible for defining software patterns and/or simulation model components that might be reused in other simulations as well as defining the whole simulation framework

- *Designer*, who is responsible for transforming the simulation model constructed by the modeler into a software design able to be more easily implemented

- *Developer*, who is responsible for implementing the model designed by the designer

- *Tester*, who is responsible for the verification and validation of the application according to the pre-established scenarios[25]

MASim is without doubt the most appropriate methodology for agent-based modeling among all that are discussed in this chapter. It was designed specifically for this purpose. Unlike other multi-agent methodologies, MASim covers not only design phases, but also development and verification; it is concerned not only with mere process but also with roles in the development team.

On the other hand, it provides no clue, except scenarios, as to how the system should be modeled. The individual steps are often just briefly described, without any specific explanations and hints, so it is questionable whether somebody can use the methodology as is. Also there are perhaps too many roles defined, because – from the author's point of view – some of their characteristics at least partially overlap (namely modeler – software architect – designer). Design of environment is not solved by the methodology. It seems as though the authors had a great concept, but did not manage to elaborate it into an

---

[25]Campos et al. 2004, pp. 4–5.

applicable methodology. Anyway, MASim is a very useful work with several good ideas, and it can be used as an inspiration for further research in methodologies for agent-based simulations.

6.9   Prometheus

Prometheus is another general-purpose methodology that belongs among the "big" and often-cited methodologies. It is – according to its authors – intended as a practical methodology; that is, it should provide everything that is needed to specify and design agent systems (not so surprising a statement, as many other methodologies often resemble an academic exercise). The methodology is detailed – it provides detailed guidance on how to perform the various steps that form the process of Prometheus.[26] It encompasses the entire process from requirements collection to detailed design.

As usual, the design process of the methodology is divided into three phases: System Specification, Architecture Design and Detailed Design.

- The *System Specification* phase begins with a rough idea and its goal is to define requirements for the system in the form of:

  – A list of goals of the system (using *goal diagram*)
  – Use Case scenarios
  – Functionalities
  – Interfaces of the system with its environment

- In *Architectural Design* phase:

  – Agent types are defined. The agent types are identified by grouping functionalities based on considerations of coupling; and these are explored using a *coupling diagram* and an agent *acquaintance diagram* (compare with Gaia methodology in the section 6.5). Once a grouping is chosen, the resulting agents are described using agent descriptors
  – Interactions between agents using interaction diagrams and interaction protocols are described. Interaction diagrams are derived from use case scenarios; and these are then revised and generalized to produce interaction protocols
  – The overall system structure is designed using *System Overview Diagram*. This diagram captures the agent types in the system, the boundaries of the system and its interfaces in terms of actions and percepts, but also in terms of data and code that is external to the system.[27]

---

[26]Winikoff and Padgham 2004, p. 217.
[27]Ibid., p. 221.

- The Detailed Design phase consists of:

  - Agents' internals including capabilities are developed. Agent overview diagrams and capability descriptors are used

  - Process diagrams are developed from interaction protocols

  - Details of capabilities in terms of other capabilities as well as events, plans and data are developed. This is done using *capability overview diagrams* and various descriptors. A key focus is developing plan sets to achieve goals and ensuring appropriate coverage.[28]

Prometheus mainly uses UML and AUML notation for its diagrams. To support Prometheus, the PDT design tool was developed and is available for free.

Prometheus is another popular and sound methodology with strong support. Like most of others it was developed as general-purpose methodology. This means it is possible to use it for agent-based simulations, but it is particularly focused on this field.

6.10   Tropos

Tropos[29] is a well-known and deeply elaborated multi-agent methodology. Unlike most other methodologies, Tropos is a "big project" with an international working group with several tens of contributors, dozens of publications, organized workshops, and so on. There are even design tools available that support this methodology.

The methodology has five main development phases: Early Requirements, Late Requirements, Architectural Design, Detailed Design, and Implementation.

- During the *Early Requirements* phase, domain stakeholders are identified and modeled as social actors, who depend on one another for goals to be achieved, plans to be performed, and resources to be furnished[30]

- During the *Late Requirements* phase, the *system* actor is introduced and all dependencies to other actors are adjusted

- *Architectural Design* defines a system's global architecture in terms of subsystems, connected through data flows and control flows. Subsystems are modeled as actors and flows are represented as dependencies. The actors are mapped onto system actors with specific capabilities

- *Detailed Design* phase works with the individual agents and aims to specify their capabilities and specifications. Although the foregoing phases are typically

---

[28]Winikoff and Padgham 2004, p. 223.
[29]Giorgini et al. 2004.
[30]Bresciani et al. 2004, p. 5.

conceptual, in the Detailed Design phase the implementation platform is usually known and can be taken into account.[31] For detailed design, UML and AUML notation can be used

- In the *Implementation phase*, the system is implemented according to the model developed in the Detailed Design phase.

Tropos models use the following entities to describe reality in the individual stages of development:

- *Actor* – actor represents an agent or its role

- *Goal* – represents strategic interests of actors. Hard goals and soft goals are distinguished, where hard goals are clearly defined and measurable and soft goals lack a clear definition

- *Plan* – is the way of doing something, especially reaching a goal

- *Resource* – physical or informational entity

- *Dependency* – the relationship between two actors when one actor depends on another one

- *Capability* – the ability of an actor to choose and execute a plan given the present situation and events

- *Belief* – is actor's knowledge of the outer world.

Tropos is a robust and complex methodology, which makes it difficult to learn. On the other hand, it is well documented and there are enough materials and design tools for Tropos available. Tropos is more concentrated on the macro level of the multi-agent simulation. It is not specifically focused on agent-based simulations, but can be used for such application.

6.11   Chapter summary

The careful reader has probably noticed that most methodologies are very similar. They usually have several phases that always include the collection of requirements, the conceptual phase and the design phase, which is already focused on the specific implementation environment. There is a various number of phases with different content, but the principles are all the same. Most methodologies are designed as general-purpose. Their authors often aimed for the widest scope of use. In reality this seems to tend towards a

---

[31] Ibid., p. 5.

high complexity of such methodologies, which is not useful for some particular means of use (e.g., agent-based simulations).

The only exception is MASim, which is a multi-agent methodology developed especially for agent-based simulations. The idea of the methodology is beneficial; however, the methodology is not elaborated enough to be instantly applicable. Due to its robustness it is focused more on larger projects. Unlike some other multi-agent methodologies, there is also a lack of evidence about a successful implementation of this methodology.

It seems there is still a space for new methodologies that would back design and development of agent-based simulations. They could be helpful for the entire field.

Chapter 7
Limits of agent-based modeling

Since the birth of the method, an enormous number of agent models have been developed in various fields of science including social sciences and economics, computer science, physics, ecology, biological sciences and others. The *Journal of Artificial Societies and Social Simulation* (JASSS) is perhaps one of the main publication resources in the field and has published a meta-analysis that has covered articles regarding agent-based models over 10 years.[1] The study indicates 294 articles about the subject matter published just in JASSS and more than 8000 related citations from other resources including *Nature*, *American Economic Review*, *Science*, *American Journal of Sociology*, *Journal of Economic Dynamics and Control*, *Journal of Political Economy* and many others. It may seem that the field is well developed and mature and that agent-based models have a wide range of applications.

However, a researcher dealing with agent-based simulations will sooner or later face certain doubts. Although there is a handful of articles, experiments and works implementing agent-based simulations successfully, and although agent-based simulations are prominently mentioned as a promising technology at least in the past ten or fifteen years, they are not known well outside the narrow ABM community, and real applications of the method beyond scientific, educational and experimental purposes are rare. Also the vast majority of tools for development of agent-based simulations come from the scientific and educational community, with just a few commercial ones. Terminology in the field is not stable so far and there are deep gaps between views of the individual authors. All these problems show that agent-based models are probably still in a phase of infancy.

This situation causes certain epistemological questions to arise. What is the connection between theory, reality and agent-based models? Are the agent-based simulations just an interesting theoretical toy in researchers' hands, or an academic exercise? Can they provide tangible results that are comparable with empirical data? How to measure the validity of the models? Can they provide real-life knowledge or are their results entirely arbitrary?

First of all it is worthwhile to consider whether such questions even matter. Is it necessary for the models to have a relationship to reality? Any kind of model used in any

---

[1] Meyer, Lorscheid, and Troitzsch 2009.

scientific field represents limited traits of reality with certain inevitable simplifications. If we accept the idea that the purpose of the representation is to allow the comprehension of the reality and the projection of its states that have not occurred yet such that results are consistent with empirical data in case the situation happens, the interconnection between the model and reality must be tangible.

Although it seems to be a simple, logical and straightforward assumption, with a closer look we can note that outside natural and technical sciences, most qualitative and quantitative methods are at least problematic. Among the social sciences, economics has perhaps the richest apparatus of formal analytical methods, developed over at least the last 100 years. Although it is able to explain past events very well, it often fails in new situations. Also the predictions of future values of qualitative indicators often resemble nothing more than crystal ball gazing, especially in turbulent times.[2] Economists frequently argue that despite the important drawbacks of the present methods, they simply have nothing better. Hence it seems the reliability of the approach is not a crucial issue.

If there is little or no need for the reliability of a model in confrontation with reality, the use of any new method in research could be justified due to four reasons. First, the method could provide more accurate results than the current methods. Second, the method could provide results of the same quality as the current methods, but with less effort. Third, the method could provide answers to the questions the existing methods cannot provide answers for. And finally, the method can accompany factors that are not treated by the present methods.

The first reason does not apply. Agent-based models probably cannot offer better results than the traditional methods, because the problem of the traditional methods is not their principal validity, but the lack of input data. Analytical and prediction methods in economics and finance are mostly based on profound theoretical grounds, but they fail because analysts do not have enough data and they need to use various subjective estimations. Economic systems also rely on the decisions of policymakers and although these can have substantial impact, they are hardly predictable and can be irrational.[3] Agent-based models can generally work with the same input data as any other models, but the relationship between input data and the model results are far less straightforward.

The second reason also does not apply. The complexity of agent-based models is enormous. The traditional methods are based on mathematical or statistical computations that are mostly relatively simple in principle and feasible these days thanks to use of computers. Researchers in economics can perform complicated computations often without the participation of other specialists. Agent-based models are, on the other hand, complex tools that require – besides the knowledge in the subject matter – at least programming skills, which often necessitates interdisciplinary teams. Moreover, their

---

[2]Makridakis, Hogarth, and Gaba 2010.
[3]Granger 2005.

computational intensity can be extreme, especially when a higher number of agents must be involved, which makes them costly if even doable. So the efficiency of agent-based models is much lower than that of the traditional mathematical and statistical methods.

Third, it is doubtful whether agent-based models can be substituted by other types of methods. Except for the analytical approach, there are various other methods (like discrete simulations or systems dynamics) that could be at least partially utilized for the same tasks.

The last criterion can apply if there is a factor that the agent-based models can take into account more than the traditional methods. The author of this book considers *space* such a factor. Analytical methods in social sciences often do not consider spatial characteristics of the issue under research. They are often not important. We can calculate the predictions of GDP or stock indices without knowledge of such characteristics like shape of the country, the physical proximity of the individual people, and so on, because it is not important for the calculation. If there is a spatial dimension of the task, it can be a reason why to employ agent-based simulations instead of the traditional methods. The advantage of agent-based models is that unlike many other analytical methods in the social sciences, it can integrate spatial characteristics of the problem easily, which can be fruitful in many particular applications. The author is quite skeptical about the usage of agent-based models in the areas that do not incorporate spatial factors, where they have to compete with other methods.

7.1   Problems of agent-based modeling

What are the reasons that prevent agent-based simulation from a wider expansion? The author can identify the following:

• Lack of confidence in the results

• Missing methodology of the development of agent-based simulations that would be easy and comprehensible

• Missing leading development frameworks for agent-based simulations

• Computational performance limitations

• Lack of awareness about the method among the public.

Other technical challenges are discussed in the article by Cioffi-Revilla.[4].

---

[4]Cioffi-Revilla 2002.

7.2   Lack of confidence

The concerns about the reliability of agent-based models as a method are sometimes tacitly but consistently present in related literature. This is evident from the number of works that are devoted to the demonstration of reliability of the method and to procedures that are developed for reliability evaluation and betterment, and the numerous works that address the problems of agent-based model replication.[5] Heine et al.[6] argue that agent-based simulations come with advantages over the traditional methods and that the danger of arbitrariness can be prevented using so called stylized facts. Boero et al.[7] or Ormerod et al.[8] deal with an empirical verification of the results of agent-based models.

Doubts about the confidence of the method are understandable. The method is based on the belief that micro behaviors of the individual agents aggregate into macro behaviors of the whole system. It could be considered, however, a reasonable assumption, that there is actually no clear causality why this should occur. The problem is linked with the inherent trait of multi-agent systems concerning emergent properties, that is the properties of the system that appear spontaneously as a byproduct of interrelationships of the system's parts. How could be anything that arises unplanned be deemed a robust enough foundation for computation of hard results? Due to the nature of the method, an analytical verification of validity is awkward and thus a statistical approach must be used. Moreover, agent-based modeling as a scientific method should allow falsification. A truly scientific method must be falsifiable; that is, it must allow a way to be disproved.[9] Falsification of agent-based modeling as a method in social sciences is a challenging task.[10]

7.3   Missing methodology for development

Methodologies for the development of multi-agent systems are discussed in depth in chapter 6. The conclusion is that there is no strong "leader" among agent methodologies and there are no methodologies except MASim that would be focused particularly on agent-based models. MASim is moreover not enough elaborated to be instantly applicable and is so robust that it would be too costly to be applied for smaller projects. Most agent-based models are therefore developed on an ad hoc basis, or some general software methodology is used.

---

[5]Wilensky and Rand 2007; Macy and Sato 2010; Zhong and Kim 2010.
[6]Heine, Meyer, and Strangfeld 2005.
[7]Boero and Squazzoni 2005.
[8]Ormerod and Rosewell 2009.
[9]Popper 1998.
[10]Schutte 2010.

A good and easy development methodology could make the process of creation of agent models easier and therefore cheaper. A missing approach to the development also complicates training of new experts in the field. A methodology is a set of best practices – proven procedures that should lead to the successful result without unnecessary mistakes. Without it, deep interdisciplinary skills are needed for the use of the method and each implementation of a reasonable system requires building it from scratch with the risk of repeating the same mistakes over and over.

A proposal for a methodology for agent-based modeling that has the ambition to help fill this gap is presented in the following chapters.

7.4 Missing leading development frameworks

There is a high number of agent-based frameworks. Low concentration of the field is related to missing widely accepted industry standards. Certain standards exist; however, they are actually not used very frequently. Everybody treats agents differently, and there are dozens of views how they should be implemented. In chapter 3 a few of them are discussed, and the list is by no means exhaustive.

The solution to this problem lies outside the scope of this book. It probably does not lie in the development of some other, better framework, but in successful applications of the existing frameworks.

7.5 Computational performance limitations

Agent-based simulations can make extreme demands on computational power.[11] Some kinds of simulations especially in social sciences require treating millions of agents for statistically confident results.[12] There are still a few agent environments that are able to support large-scale agent-based simulations consisting of millions and more agents.[13]

Although it could seem that there is nothing complicated for high-performance computing these days, and that tools for distributed computing like clusters and grids could be used easily for the needs of a task of any size, the contrary is true. The architecture of multi-agent systems, particularly the intensive interaction between the agents, imposes special requirements that cannot be met easily by traditional techniques and the performance requirements cannot be scaled linearly.[14] Unlike other kinds of distributed information systems, the individual agents communicate permanently. Obviously, the communication between the agents running within one part of the system is much faster

---

[11]Greenough et al. 2010.
[12]Šalamon 2008b.
[13]Yamamoto, Tai, and Mizuta 2007.
[14]North et al. 2008.

than the communication between the agents in different parts. Because the physical design of the system should not influence the simulated environment, this property represents a serious obstacle.

One possible solution is the use of supercomputers,[15] but these are available just to a few cutting-edge scientific labs, so it is hardly generally feasible. Distributed systems use various partitioning techniques to overcome the problem.[16] If an agent-based model involves a certain natural scattering of agents, for example according to their spatial proximity,[17] it could be used as a basis for partitioning. This approach, however, is not without problems, as the distribution of the agents in the virtual space is seldom even and steady. A novel approach to the affordable solution of the problem is the use of graphical processors[18] for computations, which could deliver near-supercomputing performance at considerably lower cost, although the method has still substantial limitations. The programming of GPUs differs from the traditional methods. It is much less comfortable, the code must be simpler and developers are prevented from using certain standard instruments (e.g., the nVidia CUDA GPU development framework is free of recursion and of function-pointers[19])). Moreover, even the most powerful graphical chips still have their performance limits, and combining them into larger network structures like clusters is by definition even a more challenging problem than in traditional computer systems.

7.6 Popularity

Lack of awareness is probably more the consequence of the previous problems than the cause. Agent-based modeling is still an issue of a limited agent community and more or less an experimental instrument, due to low confidence in results and problems with their development. The commercial implementations are rare and there is perhaps no remarkable application that would promote them. It is a vicious circle, because the method could hardly become more popular without confidence in its results and without available tools and methodologies for development. The only option is probably slow painstaking work that would gradually promote agent-based models and prove its suitability for certain applications.

---

[15]Stroud et al. 2007.
[16]Wang et al. 2009.
[17]Šišlák, Volf, and Pěchouček 2010.
[18]Lysenko and D'Souza 2008.
[19]*nVidia GPU Programming Guide* 2005.

7.7 Spatial factors in agent-based modeling

It seems that agent-based models that incorporate spatial factors (e.g., various traffic simulations) are more successful and more common than the models without such factors; although a thorough meta-search must be performed to confirm or reject the hypothesis. On the basis of a preliminary search it appears that:

- Agent-based models are cited more often with spatial factors than without them.

- The models developed and used outside the narrow scientific community are almost exclusively space-oriented.

A possible explanation could be that spatial factors represent the added value that agent-based models can offer over other comparable methods. Furthermore, models that include spatial factors are more easily verifiable, because of their intuitive nature, and their results are more comprehensible due to easy visualization. This brings a better confidence in results. Particularly in the case of traffic models, a lower number of agents typically is needed, so the complexity of the model is more manageable.

Due to these factors it is easier to promote, among the public, agent-based models incorporating spatial factors than their other implementations. This could be perhaps the way they could increase in popularity.

7.8 Chapter summary

Agent-based modeling is a novel methodology with the potential to be used in a wide range of applications in many fields of science. However, unlike many other researchers in the field of agent-based modeling, the author does not consider the method mature and fully adopted. There are still serious practical problems that prevent it from regular implementation and much wider use. Besides technical obstacles, there are methodical and fundamental problems such as a lack of confidence in the results, missing methodology for development of agent-based simulations that would be easy and comprehensible, missing leading development frameworks for agent-based simulations, computational performance limitations and a lack of information about the method among the public. It seems that the best opportunity to succeed rests with agent-based models that involve spatial factors, because unlike many other methods the agent-based models offer instruments for easily incorporating them.

Chapter 8

Agentology

The rise of methodologies for development of information systems has allowed faster, cheaper and less risky software development processes and increased the quality of the final software. It is a pervasive idea in the agent research community that one of the key issues in the transition of agents from research to industrial practice is the need for a mature software engineering methodology for the specification and design of agent systems. Although there are several agent methodologies available (see chapter 6), the subfield of agent-based simulations is not sufficiently taken into account. The only relevant methodology focused specifically on design of agent-based simulations is MASim, and its limitations as discussed in section 6.8 make it difficult to apply. The author of this book considers there is a demand for a new methodology that would support the development of agent-based models specifically.

The response for the aforementioned demand is Agentology, the methodology for the development of agent-based models. The overview of such methodology is contained in this chapter. The methodology was developed during the work on several agent-based simulations and tested on various projects over two years. Even though there is indeed still room for further development (as in the case of any methodology), Agentology can be readily applied.

Should any methodology be useful for users and have a chance for spreading, it has to fulfill several characteristics, identified as the following. The methodology should be:

- Easily trainable

- Immediately applicable

- Independent of any specific technology, language or environment

- Universal

- Freely available

Easily trainable means that the methodology must be simple and intuitive insofar as users should be able to learn it quickly and seamlessly. Unlike general software development methodologies, in the case of agent-based models, the participants are not only developers and other IT-professionals, but also experts from other fields (economics, statistics, etc.). For that purpose, Agentology is specific and provides concrete hints and examples and takes non-IT participants into account. It was inspired by the best practices and good ideas contained in several other methodologies, so it is easy to digest. There is indeed always a risk that a simple methodology that is lacking a rigorous procedure could leave more freedom for their users than would be desirable for delivery of high-quality output. This argument was taken into account; however, "easy trainability" and simplicity was still considered of a higher value in this case.

Immediately applicable means that there should be no further obstacles to apply the methodology by trained staff. In fact, for any new methodology, there can be a problem with a lack of tools that would support it. Many multi-agent methodologies solve this problem by providing particular tools (e.g., Prometheus[1] offers the PDT design tool[2]). However, such an approach brings many setbacks. Development of any new design tool is costly, the tools must be supported, users must be trained not only for the methodology, but also for the tool, and so on. A better solution is using the existing and widely available tools for a new methodology. This is the path Agentology takes. No specific tools are required, users can use project management tools that they use with other methodologies and all models can be developed with the tools that support UML. It does not mean Agentology uses UML as its modeling language, but Agentology's diagrams are based on UML artifacts.

Independence is necessary for any methodology that is not connected with any specific product and has ambitions to be widely implemented. Agentology is independent of any agent paradigm, any framework, any technology and any programming language. The first part of the development is performed on a conceptual level and the platform-specific aspects are not considered until it is inevitable. This principle is often called the "Principle of three architectures" (P3A).[3]

Universal means that the methodology should encompass any purpose and any size of the agent-based model. Agentology fulfills this requirement mainly by a strict distinction between the conceptual and platform-specific part of the design.

Free availability is important for the methodology to be spread and generally used and is not connected with any influential organization. Agentology is publicly available under the CCPL license.[4]

The whole methodology is basically a process of a repetitive transformation of models into more detailed ones. The process starts with an economic model (or a model from other fields) of reality, which is transformed into a conceptual model of the multi-agent system, which is transformed into a platform-specific model, which is transformed into

---

[1] Winikoff and Padgham 2004, p. 217.
[2] See http://www.cs.rmit.edu.au/agents/pdt (visited on 11.3.2010)
[3] Řepa 1999.
[4] See http://creativecommons.org (visited on 27.11.2009)

the final agent-based model. The purpose of the methodology is to make the transition among the individual steps easy and seamless.

8.1 Roles

For better orientation, several roles of team members for the whole development process were derived. It does not mean that so many people must work on each project. Role does not imply any specific person, but a set of competencies. Multiple roles, or even all roles, can be performed by the same person, as is very common especially for smaller tasks. On the other hand, one role can be indeed played by more than one person.

The *Expert* plays a crucial role in the very beginning and the end of the project. Experts assign the task and serve as sources of knowledge about the subject matter. They provide the information for the statement of the task to analysts. At the end of the project experts evaluate the results of the experiments conducted using the simulation and test it for its consistency with reality. The required competence of the expert is the expertise in the respective field..

The *Analyst*'s duty is the elicitation of knowledge from the expert and the definition of the task as a problem that can be solved using computer-aided techniques. The analyst should be able to distinguish what is important and what is less important and formulate the task into the form that is pertinent for further elaboration. The analyst should have an adequate knowledge of the subject matter and a certain level of technical skills. He should have good communication skills.

The *Modeler*'s job is to turn the defined task into a conceptual (platform independent) model represented by a graphical modeling language. The modeler should know the modeling techniques and language and should be able to use modeling tools. He does not need a special knowledge in the modeled field; however he must be able to comprehend the task definition.

The *Platform specialist* participates in the selection of the platform that will be used for the implementation of the model. After the platform is selected, he turns the conceptual model into the platform-specific one. Platform specialists need skills in agent conceptual modeling and a deep knowledge of technical details of agent platforms. They should be familiar with the methods of modeling and programming of agent-based simulations on the current platform.

The *Programmer* develops code of the simulation on the current platform. The programmer needs to comprehend design models and needs good technical skills on the current agent platform. He should be aware of development environments and development and debugging procedures on the platform.

The *Tester*'s task is to test the developed model and its components during the development phase, in cooperation with programmers, as well as to perform the model evaluation as the final step of the whole process, in cooperation with experts. Testers should have adequate knowledge and technical skills on the current platform, should know testing procedures of multi-agent systems and should be able to obtain satisfactory knowledge of the subject matter.

8.2   Design and development process

The design and development process in Agentology consists of four phases and nine steps. Each step works with the results of the previous one, so the process has the structure of a successive or iterative (colloquially known as waterfall) approach.[5] In an ideal case, it should not be necessary to go back in the process; however, in practical application, it is often inevitable to return and make adjustments in a part of the work that was already closed down.

- Phase 1 – Requirements definition

    - Step 1 – Task formulation
    - Step 2 – Task evaluation

- Phase 2 – Conceptual model

    - Step 3 – Conceptual modeling
    - Step 4 – Consistency check

- Phase 3 – Platform-specific model

    - Step 5 – Selection of a development platform
    - Step 6 – Transformation guide
    - Step 7 – Platform-specific model

- Phase 4 – Simulation model

    - Step 8 – Development, debugging and testing
    - Step 9 – Model evaluation

All steps are not of the same importance. This methodology is intended to be able to cover a project of any size from a school exercise to a large scientific project. Obviously, the same methodology can hardly fit all sizes of project as is. For smaller and easier projects it could be simplified. Particularly steps 2, 4, 6 and 7 can be omitted and steps 3 and 9 can be abridged. The process of Agentology is depicted in Figure 8.1.

---

[5]Royce 1970.

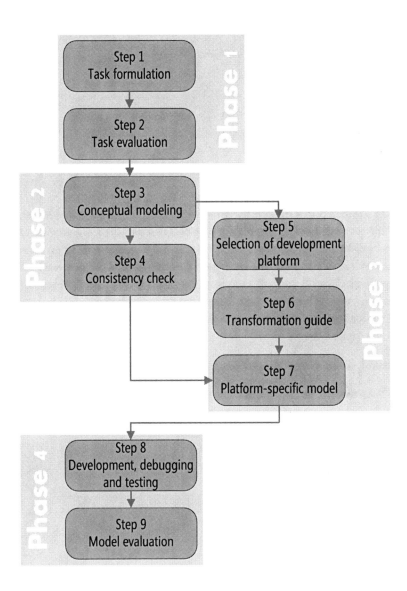

Figure 8.1 – Process of Agentology. Steps 1, 7, and 8 are mandatory; steps 3 and 9 could be abridged, and steps 2, 4, 5, and 6 are recommended.

8.2.1   Step 1 – Task formulation

Goal	to specify the task in formal way that should provide sufficient information for the development of the simulation in the following steps
Output	task specification – the model of simulated situation
Participants	analyst, expert

The aim of this step is to formulate the problem that will be solved with the agent-based model. The simulated reality is typically very complex and the assignment is often too vague to be solved as is. For that reason it is crucial to perform this step responsibly. The result of this step should be a simplified description of simulated reality. The analyst should describe all relevant aspects of the object matter and distinguish what is important and what is less important. The goals of the simulation should be set in order to avoid simulation just for simulation's sake (which can be sometimes the case).

Task description should cover mainly the following topics:

- Overall description of the problem

- What processes can be identified in the problem

- The entities engaged in the processes – people, companies, organizations, vehicles, machines, groups, animals, and so on

- What the entities want

- What the entities do

- What are the characteristics of the entities

- How the entities affect each other

- How the environment looks – its spatial characteristics, its temporal characteristics and other attributes

- How the environment affects the entities

- How the entities affect the environment

- What is the purpose of the task

- What do we measure, what are the metrics

- What is the question we answer

- How to evaluate the developed model

- Testing criteria.

The task is typically in an open text, but it can include other components like mathematical formulae, schemes, charts and other kinds of diagrams (the Use Case diagram from UML can be convenient in some cases). All the materials must be comprehensible for all further participants on the project, which may not include the experts on the subject matter, but the computer science professionals.

The output of this step is rendered by the analyst, who draws from relevant literature and other sources and gathers knowledge from experts, customers and other stakeholders, typically using structured interviews and consultations.

The analyst must adopt reasonable simplifications. The result of this phase is a model in economic (or other analogous) terms; that is, the reality is modeled with a simplified textual description, mathematical functions, equations, charts, and so on. The model should be ample enough for further elaboration, because the team members that work with it in the later steps can (and probably will) lack information about the subject matter. It is indeed seldom feasible to anticipate all the contingencies beforehand, so it is expected that refinements will be inevitable in the further steps; however, the model should be as good as possible, because it is much cheaper to avoid errors in the earlier phases than in the later ones.

The analyst should neglect the fact that he or she is working on an agent-based simulation, for now. So far it is an economical problem, a traffic problem, and so on, and not an issue from the realm of computer science. The aim in this step is to set the task that should be solved anyway, no matter the method that will be finally used. Less experienced modelers can sometimes tend to presuppose the method (e.g., agent-based modeling) and automatically count on using it even if the problem should be treated with another method more efficiently. In this step, there should be no agents, no behaviors and so on mentioned, and the analyst should focus solely on the problem, as the process of its resolution will be worked out in further steps. The purpose of this step is to set the problem in a certain formal way, not to solve it.

The criteria for the assessment of the developed model should be included. They will be used in the last step of the whole process to check whether the model is in conformance with reality.

In the following box there is an example of task formulation of a simple problem. The real problems would be described in a more complex and more detailed manner; however the basic approach is indeed the same.

Example

This is a traffic simulation with the goal to compare the efficiency of human traffic controllers with automated traffic control using traffic lights.

We simulate an intersection in a city with two crossing streets. Each street is wide enough for one lane in both directions. There are two kinds of vehicles on the streets: cars and trucks. Vehicles come to the intersection randomly from random directions in random intervals (from Poisson distribution with a mean of 10). They have random initial speeds – normal distribution (50; 15). They adjust their speeds according to the traffic (they try to avoid crashes) and according to the signals of the policeman (traffic controller). All kinds of vehicles can change their speeds by 5 per second. Vehicles cannot overtake each other.

Vehicles can crash. It happens if two vehicles find themselves in one moment in the same place. A car crash causes damage to both cars at a certain level. A measure of the crash is a number between 0% and 100% where 0% means no damage and 100% means total damage. The level of damage is a function of vectors of their speeds (1 minus a ratio of the absolute value of the sum of vectors to the sum of absolute values of vectors):

$$d = 1 - \frac{\sqrt{(x_1 + x_2)^2 + (y_1 + y_2)^2}}{\sqrt{x_1^2 + y_1^2} + \sqrt{x_2^2 + y_2^2}}, \tag{8.1}$$

$$x_1 = v_1 \cos \varphi_1, \tag{8.2}$$

$$y_1 = v_1 \sin \varphi_1, \tag{8.3}$$

$$x_2 = v_2 \cos \varphi_2, \tag{8.4}$$

$$y_2 = v_2 \sin \varphi_2, \tag{8.5}$$

where v_1 is the speed of vehicle 1, φ_1 is the direction (course) of vehicle 1, v_2 is the speed of vehicle 2 and φ_2 is a direction (course) of vehicle 2. Any damage higher than 70% is total. In that case, the vehicle "disappears" in 1 hour. Any damage lower than 10% is immaterial and then the vehicle can continue. Damage between 10 and 70% means a delay of half an hour and the vehicle can then go on. If there is a damaged car on the road, other cars must go around. Vehicles cannot run over the policeman.

If traffic is controlled by a policeman, he watches the situation and shows a go signal to the direction where the longest queue is and a stop signal to the others. If he shows a signal, he does not change it before 20 seconds elapses. If traffic is controlled by lights, they switch every 30 seconds, no matter the current situation. Cars may or may not obey the signals. In 1% of cases they will ignore a stop signal. If the car is already in the intersection and the signal is changed, it will continue regardless of the signal.

The simulation lasts for one simulation day.

Research problems   The simulation should answer the following problems:

- What is an average length of queues in both situations?

- What is more efficient way of traffic control (policeman vs. lights)?

Testing criteria   The queues should be dynamically stable, meaning that they could grow and shrink repeatedly, but they must not grow all the time.

8.2.2   Step 2 – Task evaluation

Goal	to assess the task created in the previous step in order to confirm that it is suitable for elaboration as an agent-based model
Output	task specification verified for the development of agent-based model
Participants	analyst, modeler

This step is optional and could be skipped as it does not bring any new contribution into the design process. It is however not recommended, because the following procedure lessens the risk of the whole development.

It could seem superfluous to check the task for whether it is suitable for agent-based modeling when the agent-based model is what we use from the very beginning. The analyst should recognize what method is the most appropriate for solving the task as early as during its definition. However, analysts could also sometimes succumb to the presupposition of making an agent-based model and sticking with it, even if some other method would be better for the particular task. Sometimes it can be difficult to discern and sometimes the original assignment could be so vague that it is hard to make a decision about the method beforehand. This step is particularly important for less experienced analysts[6] who are often less sensitive about the pertinence of the method.

Anyway, now is the right time to stop and check the task deeply in this way, because any further steps will bring certain costs that would be wasted if we discovered in the later steps that we had chosen an inconvenient method.

---

[6]For instance the students working on their first agent-based models.

There are indeed no strict rules for how to distinguish whether it is a task for an agent-based model or not, and sometimes the question is hard to answer conclusively. However, several indicators have been discovered that can help make the decision more reliable.

- *Are there entities that can make decisions?* Agents are defined as autonomous decision-making entities. In other kinds of simulation methods, the entities – if even represented individually – are mostly passive.

- *Are there many kinds of decision-making entities or many kinds of decisions?* Perhaps all simulation methods are able to represent decision-making. However, the methods that are based on a top-down principle (discrete simulation, system dynamics) can struggle if there are many decisions or decision-making entities, because their "global" algorithms or equations could be too complex. The agent-based model is built bottom-up and consists of numerous entities that can be very simple, and the development of each of them could be simple too.

- *Does it look as if the system will have dynamic characteristics? In other words, do its former states influence future ones?* Various methods have various abilities to treat the dynamics of the system. Discrete simulation is relatively weak on this issue. System dynamics can operate on a macro level using differential equations. Agent-based models consist of entities (agents) that can have memory where they can store even very complex data that can steer their behavior in the future on the basis of their previous experience, making this method very strong for the representation of model dynamics.

- *We do not feel a need to treat an overall behavior of the whole system on a macro level.* Agent-based modeling is based on a bottom-up principle. There is actually no "macro level" of the simulation that could be influenced directly by the developers. All changes, parameters and tuning of the model are being done through the agents on a micro level. If the requirements for the model are too macro-oriented, it could be a signal that agent-based modeling is not a proper method.

- *Is it difficult to describe the whole situation as a process (or activity) diagram or state-transition diagram?* The process model is a typical macro-level view. As mentioned above, agent-based models are oriented to the micro level. The best method for process-oriented problems is often discrete simulation.

- *Is it difficult to "count up" the entities into lump sums and then work solely with such amounts? That is, are there many different entities that we cannot treat together?* If we can count the entities up and instead of working with the individual agents we can work efficiently with several mathematical functions or equations that describe their sets, other methods like discrete simulation or system dynamics could be a better choice because they are often simpler.

- *Are spatial factors of the environment important for the simulation?* If this indicator is positive, it very likely means that an agent-based model is suitable; however, if there are no spatial factors, it says nothing about its appropriateness. The ability to encompass the spatial factors is a particular strength of agent-based models over other simulation methods. As each agent is represented individually, it can hold such parameters like position, size, speed, and so on. very easily and their spatial interaction could be hence implemented quite naturally.

If we can answer in the affirmative for all or the majority of the foregoing questions, it is very likely that we have an assignment for the agent-based model. Otherwise, a deeper inspection and consideration of other alternatives would be desirable. We can move back to step 1 and refine the task or recommend using another technique.

Example

We can analyze the previous task according to the rules recommended in this step:

- There are entities that make decisions – vehicles and a policeman.

- There are just two kinds of decision making entities, but they can make many kinds of decisions (especially vehicles – direction, speed, whether to obey signals or not, avoiding obstacles, etc.).

- There are dynamic characteristics in the system – cars have to avoid obstacles, damaged cars, etc.

- It is hard to treat the system on its macro level. There is no single process and every entity has its own characteristics (direction, speed, destination, etc.).

- We can draw activity diagrams and state-transition diagrams of the particular entities, but we can hardly render them for the whole situation.

- Each entity has its unique variables and makes decisions based on them. The only "global" values are the policeman's signals.

- Spatial characteristics of the environment are very important.

We can see that the vast majority of conditions is satisfied including the last one – spatial characteristics – which is a very strong indicator. Thus, the task seems to be suitable for an agent-based solution (as traffic models often are).

8.2.3   Step 3 – Conceptual modeling

Goal	to transform the task into a conceptual model of the system that consists of the set of diagrams
Output	conceptual; that is, a platform-independent model of the system
Participants	modeler

So far we have worked with the requirements or assignment of the task. This is the first step, when the team can move to the mere solution. The modeler's mission is to transform the requirements into the description of structure and behavior of the developed system. As in other software methodologies, most of the model description is made using diagrams in formal graphical language that makes the structure more comprehensible, lucid and the information more accurate than an open text. However, not all necessary information can be always captured in the diagrams, and that is why modelers should add textual notes everywhere, as it is indispensable for right understanding.

The model is strictly conceptual in this step. It means that it is not bound with any specific language, agent paradigm, framework, tool, platform or any other concrete technology. The purpose of the conceptual model is to take down all required features of the multi-agent system that solve the assigned task, no matter how the system will be later developed technically. It should be theoretically possible to implement the system that is described by the conceptual model on any technology. Such a distinction is common in many software methodologies and it is very convenient, because the modeler can focus on the solution in this step and can omit the specific limitations resulting from the choice of any particular technology. Although it is often practically not possible, the optimum technology should be always selected according to the needs of the model, but the model should not be adjusted according to the abilities of the technology. If we assume that the most feasible model for the current task is developed in this step, it implies that every change that is enforced by the abilities of the technology must make the model worse. It is indeed often practically necessary to make several tradeoffs, but if so, they should be made in later phases of the project.

The process of creating the conceptual model is described in the following paragraphs using Agentology's conceptual modeling diagrams. It is recommended for the purposes of the development of the conceptual model; however, it can be replaced with other language that would seem appropriate for the purpose. The model consists of several diagrams (they are described in chapter 8.3 in detail) that depict various aspects of the system. The diagrams are partially redundant to the extent that they describe the same reality from different views and together they create the big picture. The modeler can follow the suggested sequence of diagrams, but it will probably be inevitable to return and adjust some of the already drawn diagrams in order to bring them into conformance with the others. Such a process is repeated over and over until the complete and internally consistent conceptual model is finished.

The recommended course of modeling is as follows.

The first step is the creation of an agent diagram on a global level (see section 8.3.1 on the page 139). We should find out all the agents that will be modeled. Agents mean agent classes in this context; that is, the abstract patterns of agent instances. If they are not apparent, a good technique for their discovery can be to underscore all nouns in the text of the task formulation and find those most common among them. These are then the candidates for agents. Another approach is to identify the distinct entities (people, businesses, machines, etc.) in the text and consider which of them should make decisions. The entity that makes decisions is probably an agent. A distinctive sign of agents are goals (see section 5.2.3); therefore if we can expect that the entity is able to have goals, it can probably be an agent. It is also possible to combine all the aforementioned approaches. The entities should be assigned an apt name. It would be practical if the agent's name is substantive and singular.[7] Each agent should have also assigned its goal(s) that can be expressed either directly in the agent diagram or in a goal diagram (see the section 8.3.1). After drawing agents we should model relationships. There can be inheritance (generalization-specialization), association and three types of interaction between agents (see chapter 5 and section 8.3.1). The global agent diagram represents the topmost level of the whole conceptual model and it is a point of departure for all future steps of the modeling process.

In the next step, an agent diagram on a detailed level (see chapter 8.3.1) is created. Detailed agent diagrams should be elaborated from the global ones. In some cases, when there are just a few simple agent classes in the system and there is no risk of misunderstanding, both levels can be merged into one joint agent diagram that combines both levels of granularity. Normally, there are as many agent diagrams on a detailed level as agents in the global agent diagram. The main elements of the detailed agent diagram are behaviors that stem from the agent's goals. Each behavior of the agent causes an action of the agent and/or change in the agent's data (otherwise there is no reason why such behavior should exist[8]). Each action of other agents or the environment applied to the agent must be handled by a behavior. Each percept can be handled by a behavior. Each behavior must be launched by some event – that is, a percept, an action or another behavior of the same agent. Using these rules, behaviors can be derived from an agent's goals and interactions. It is practical to describe behaviors with gerunds to underscore their

---

[7]Analogous to classes in the class diagram in object-oriented programming.
[8]This is a signal that the behavior and/or agent's data should be reconsidered.

persistence, which is what distinguishes them from object methods that are executed instantly. Interactions should be named with the noun that expresses what information is transferred. The caption should be unique in the entire model. Behaviors are typically added first in order to connect the agent with its surroundings. Then datastores and other behaviors can be included, and finally all the elements should be interconnected with the internal dataflows.

The next diagram that is added into a model is often an environment diagram (see section 8.3.1). The process of construction of the diagram is the same as the process of construction of a detailed agent diagram. First, there must be behaviors that back any kind of interaction of the environment (action, percept), then other interactions and datastores are derived and all the elements are interconnected.

As soon as the agent diagrams are finished, we continue to design its components using particle diagrams. The common process is to elaborate the defined behaviors using activity diagrams that can describe behaviors' functionalities (see section 8.3.2 for details). During this job, further pieces of knowledge can emerge that will be incorporated into class diagrams and communication diagrams and into the improvements of activity diagrams or even the existing agent diagrams.

More specifically, we should create class diagrams for all datastores and interactions except communications (but there can be class diagrams for their individual messages). Modelers should always bear in mind that the model ought to remain conceptual – that is, platform-independent – in this phase. This means that the structure of data should be described generally and modelers have to avoid data types where possible. We should consider that agent-based system development is much different from that which is object-based. Object-oriented design and programming is a relatively mature paradigm where almost everything important has been already defined and there are clear contingencies between the conceptual model, platform-specific model and code. In agent-oriented design and programming however, such is not yet the case. As mentioned in the foregoing chapters, there are often a bunch of concepts for almost any single aspect of the system in agent-oriented programming. If we store data in an agent, we can use regular objects and classic data structures or we can use logical facts; or we do not even need to store data at all if we decide to develop a purely reactive system (see chapter 3.3). Class diagrams are bound particularly with an object-oriented world, so we can be tempted to see our system as object-oriented as well, but that is not a good mindset. Class diagrams in Agentology describe a concept of the entity; mainly what data should be stored. There should be less stipulated about how the data should be stored, as the modeler is supposed almost to avoid data types, scopes and so on if it is not particularly necessary. Operations (methods) could be defined if needed, but any platform-specific characteristics have to be omitted as well.

The next step is to elaborate communication-interactions if there are any in the model. For each communication, there should be a communication diagram (see section 8.3.2). Note that communication that is depicted in the communication diagrams is composed of the individual messages which should often have also corresponding class diagrams.

The last part of the conceptual analysis is a design of the user environment and the output of the simulation model. Few software methodologies cope with the user environment of applications. This is probably in part due to to the difficulty of depicting the user environment comprehensibly, and in part due to the fact that the user environment is highly standardized today and the need for its modeling is limited. In agent-based simulations such is not the case. The output of the model can range from simple numeric values over different charts to complex visualizations of output. The visualization of the output could be sometimes more difficult and challenging to develop than the mere agent-based model, and so it is an important factor of the intricacy (and cost) of the whole process. In order to avoid any further misrepresentations, there always should be enclosed characteristics and sketches of the user environment or output of the model. There is no specific notation for the environment, but the modeler should always provide enough materials that should be clear to all participants in the further phases of the project. Each element of the scheme should be assigned a specification from where it draws data that it displays. If there is displayed, for instance, a figure representing an agent, it should be clear from which data structure it gets its coordinates, direction, pace, size and other relevant characteristics. Such specification must be indeed consistent with the names of elements in other diagrams of the model.

To sum up, the recommended method of conceptual design is shown in Figure 8.2. A global agent diagram is created as the first step, supported eventually by a goal diagram. Then agent diagrams on the detailed level and environment diagrams are derived from it. They contain behaviors, datastores and relationships. For behaviors, activity diagrams should be drawn. There should be class diagrams for datastores, all kinds of actions and percepts, and communication diagrams should be created for communications. Finally, there should be added class diagrams for the individual messages of the communication diagrams.

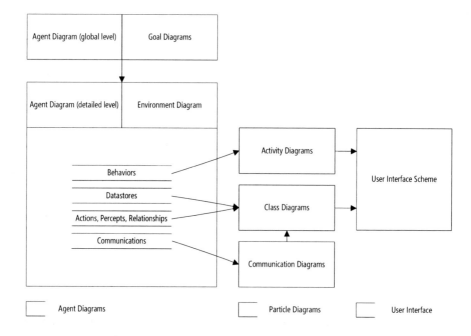

Figure 8.2 – Scheme of conceptual design process

8.2.4   Step 4 – Consistency check

Goal	to assess the consistency of the conceptual model in order to confirm that it is suitable for a further elaboration as a platform-specific model
Output	a conceptual model verified for the development of the platform-specific model
Participants	modeler

This step is optional, and could be skipped as it does not bring any new contribution into the design process. However it is strongly recommended to perform the check, because the following procedure lessens the risk of the process. Skipping the consistency check could save some time in this phase, but it could be significantly outweighed by the problems and modifications in the future ones.

As mentioned above, the conceptual model consists of a set of individual diagrams that represent various views of the same thing: the solution. Consistency means that these diagrams are compatible, the model is internally coherent and that everything "fits together." It is very important for the model to be consistent, because an inconsistent model cannot be developed into a code and will require making changes later. The more advanced the phase of the project, the more costly are any changes, so it is advised to check the model beforehand in order to avoid further troubles. Especially more complex models can be puzzling, and the easy method offered in this step could be a good instrument to check it. On the other hand, even if this technique can unveil a great deal of potential problems, there can still remain some that cannot be solved this way.

The consistency check is based essentially on a comparison of occurrences of related elements in different diagrams. Because the determining phenomenon of the agent world is interaction, it is the focal point of the method as well. The following technique is described in the way it can be used manually. It is possible and highly desirable for it to be automated by functions of CASE tools in the future.

The first step is to write down all the interactions occurring in all kinds of our diagrams. Every interaction should be included only once, even if it is present in more than one diagram. Then we draw a *consistency table* with the following columns: interaction, agent diagram, behavior, class diagram, related behavior, communication. We put the list of interactions into the *interaction* column of the table.

For each item in the interaction column we add the name of the agent having the interaction and the name of the behavior handling the interaction in the agent diagram into the respective columns. Then we write down the name of the class diagram representing the interaction into the next columns. If it is a communication, we write the name of the communication diagram instead. The name of the behavior covering the interaction on the other side should be written into the last column. In the case of actions and percepts, the related behavior is typically a certain behavior of the environment (environment diagram) and in the case of other interactions it is a behavior of another agent (agent diagram).

Strictly logically, interactions between two agents (an agent's actions applied to other agents and communications) should be included twice – from the points of view of both agents – but we include them just once for practical reasons. If the same interaction (the same name and content) appears multiple times in the model (i.e., several kinds of agents perform the same interaction), it should be included as many times as in the model.

Each item recorded in the table should be marked off in the respective diagram in order to avoid duplication.

At the end, for each interaction the whole row in the table should be filled and all entities in all diagrams except datastores, some internal behaviors and messages in communication diagrams should be marked so that the model is internally consistent. Finally, goal diagrams should be checked, once for each "asterisk in brackets" (see section 8.3.1).

The resulting table is perhaps surprisingly of relatively low importance. What is important in this process is not the result, but the process of its creation when the diagrams are being checked. The process of the consistency check need not be strictly followed; the tables can be adjusted according to the particular needs of the project. The tuning of the diagrams, their reconciliation and making them "fit together" is what is pivotal in this step, rather than the exact way to reach it.

Example

The following is a consistency table for the example with the intersection that was used in the foregoing sections. In the first column are interactions. We can see "viewpoint" twice in the column, because this interaction relates to two agents (it does not matter that the same class is used). In the AD column there are names of agents adhering to the respective interactions that are present in the agent diagram (note that the Policeman agent is marked with an asterisk – this just denotes that there is no such diagram (detailed) in this book and it has no meaning in a regular analysis). In the next column, there is a behavior participating in the current interaction. In the CD column we can see names of classes related to the interactions or the name of a communication diagram (Signals) that unfortunately also cannot be found in the book. Finally, there are the behaviors on the other side of the respective interaction (i.e., the environment's behaviors or the behaviors of the other agents).

Table 8.1 – An example of a consistency table: The Intersection. The entities marked with an asterisk cannot be found in the examples in this chapter.

relationship	AD	behavior	CD	rb
viewpoint	Vehicle	Traffic Observation	Viewpoint	View Rendition
viewpoint	Policeman*	Traffic Observation*	Viewpoint	View Rendition
damage	Vehicle	Damage Processing	Damage	Collision Processing
move	Vehicle	Vehicle Control	Move	Move Processing
traffic signals	Vehicle	Signal Reception	Signals*	Signaling*

8.2.5 Step 5 – Selection of a development platform

Goal	to select a concrete platform, approach, language and other specific technological aspects for the development of the agent-based model
Output	decision about the platform
Participants	modeler, platform specialist

So far, the model was developed as a concept, without link-up to any specific platform, system, framework, technology or language. It is very useful for the initial phase when we specify how the model will look and how it will work. However, in a certain moment, it is necessary to switch to a concrete platform, technology, and so on in order to call the idea into action. The chosen platform should be indeed the best feasible for our purposes and needs.

We typically have to choose:

- *platform* – an agent framework or library (a decision about developing an original platform for the project is also a valid option)

- *programming language* – this decision is typically closely adherent to the choice of the platform

- agent *approach* – as discussed in chapter 3, there are many kinds of agents and many approaches to how they can be implemented. Some platforms are particularly developed for a certain kind of agent whilst the others can support any approach needed.

- *technology* – hardware and software. It is often given by the selected platform as well.

As we can see, the platform seems to be a determining element of the selection of the specific environment for the development of an agent-based simulation. However, sometimes we can have such strong arguments for using a specific programming language or technology that it must be taken into consideration in choosing a platform. From now on, if not stated otherwise, "platform" will be used as a unifying term for all of the aforementioned technological aspects.

We should always assess the current state of agent technologies in this phase. Unlike other kinds of software, agents and related matters are not a mature technology yet.

Developers of the agent system then should not settle for the systems they know, but should conduct a research for the current situation.

The choice of the right platform is not an easy task. The following structured process containing a set of questions could help:

- *What is the size of the project?* Size seems to be a crucial characteristic of any agent model. There can be two meanings of "size." One is the overall complexity of the model – the number of kinds of agents, the number of their interactions, intricacy of their behaviors, and so on. This typically poses little problem for use of the model, but it is an issue for its development. The more complex the model, the more difficult it is to build, and then the platforms with advanced development tools should be used. The latter meaning of "size" is the number of agents participating in the simulation. As discussed in section 7.5 the number of agents is the main limiting factor for agent-based modeling, and the development of models with a huge number of agents could be extremely complicated. There are just a very few agent frameworks that support large agent-based simulations and even so, most such mega-scale agent-based simulations are developed on a special platform created for the particular purpose. If we plan such a model, we should think about its simplification, and if it is not possible, our spectrum of frameworks is very limited or it will even be necessary to develop an original platform for the purpose. For smaller projects there is a wide variety of options.

- *What output do we need?* The sophistication of output could be a limiting factor in the selection of agent platform, because their abilities vary. Some platforms have no special libraries for any output beyond raw data. Others are focused especially on visualization and offer, for example, libraries for 3D rendering, video making, and so on. Unfortunately, this often comes at the expense of computing abilities. Developer and analyst must decide according to the consumer's requirements for the result. If we need just scientific data, there will be probably no special needs for a "nice" output and we have plenty of options. If the output is intended for public and/or popular presentation, the sophisticated visualization can be very valuable and then the set of possibilities is much narrower. In special cases, the output can be solved separately. The simulation can provide data that can be visualized using an independent application.

- *Do we need certain extraordinary characteristics of the platform?* There are already many platforms focused on a particular area of agent-based simulations. There are, for example, special platforms for traffic simulation, ecology, education purposes, and so on. This could be helpful in that such platforms can already contain properties that should be developed separately in any general-purpose platform. It can save our time and let us focus on the important factors of the model. On the other hand, the particular features may or may not fit our needs, and they often contain specific experience and "best practice" of their authors that do not always meet our needs and expectations.

- *What skills do our developers have?* This is often the determining factor, because we often simply choose the technology that our project staff can use. Such a decision is mostly rational, as training for any new technology is costly. On the other hand, according to the development of the industry, the technology that our developers know is not necessarily the best for our purposes. The benefits the technology could bring can sometimes outweigh the cost of training on a new platform. However, many platforms in the agent world use the same or similar concepts; some stem from others, and therefore the training need not be too complicated.

- *Does the platform support required features?* There are dozens of platforms available that differ markedly. Some of them are focused particularly on a certain purpose, such as educational. Therefore they contain different palettes of functionalities they can offer. With the knowledge of the conceptual model, developers should preferably avoid the platforms where the needed feature is not directly supported. It is mostly possible to implement any requirement stemming from the conceptual model somehow, but sometimes it is only at large expense. Developers should indeed choose among such platforms that fit the needs of the conceptual model best.

- *How is the chosen platform supported and how will it be supported in the future?* If we have already made a choice and narrowed the set of options, we should assess them. Support for the individual platforms varies. Some of them are well supported, with plenty of materials, manuals, discussion forums, conferences and a wide community of users. Some are often just a result of scholarly research where the support is poor. Using such platforms is a problem in case we face difficulties during the process. One point to consider is the present support of the platform and another is its support in the future. Amazingly, the future support of the technology is often not so hot an issue in agent-based simulations as in the case of other software applications, because the simulations are often developed as one-shot or one-purpose systems, and after they fulfill their goals, there is no need to support them anymore. Designers should always consider whether the system will be used for a longer time and if there will be a need to support it in future.

The choice of the right platform is very important because if the decision proves later to be wrong, a lot of value that would be produced in the further steps could be wasted. If a new platform is selected that developers have a little experience with, it is worth testing a few prototypes with the particular problems of the planned model first.

8.2.6   Step 6 – Transformation guide

Goal	to develop a method for the transformation of the conceptual model into a platform-specific model or a program code for given platform
Output	transformation guide
Participants	platform specialist

This step is optional and could be skipped if there is already experience with the platform used.

The process of design of a platform-specific model of agent-based simulation is hard to describe generally, due to low standardization in this field. The whole concept of object-oriented programming is deeply standardized after decades of its development and there is a stable body of norms, patterns and rules. Each object-oriented language offers more or less the same palette of basic principles of object-oriented programming and therefore it can be easily supported with various methodologies, development tools, and so on.

In the agent world the situation is much more difficult, because the level of its standardization is markedly lower. Virtually every agent framework uses its own concept of agency and it is technically built mostly on an object-oriented language.

In such a situation there can be described no universal method for the transition of the conceptual model into a platform-specific model. This step is about how to develop a method that will be used for the transformation of the conceptual model into a concrete model for a specific platform chosen in the foregoing step. It is also possible to decide to skip the platform-specific model and transform the conceptual model directly into the programming code. Then the guide should give a clue how to do it. In the case of simpler simulations, especially in a situation with experienced developers, it is possible to consider skipping these steps altogether and transforming the conceptual model directly into the program code without any methodology. Risks and costs of such a decision must be taken into account. Particularly in the case that developers have only limited experience with the specific platform, it is desirable to perform this step in full.

If there is already no such method from the previous projects, it has to be developed. Designers should render a transformation guide that is a manual describing transformation of every kind of element utilized in the conceptual model into the platform-specific model. Because a vast majority of agent frameworks contain object-oriented architecture, the transformation of agent class diagrams and activity diagrams is relatively simple. In most cases there can be almost a one-to-one transformation into UML object diagrams.

In the case of agent diagrams, the problem is trickier, because there are no general counterparts in the object-oriented world. Designers must seek the equivalent concepts in the particular platform that can be used for the representation of the respective conceptual elements. If there are no such things, similar concepts must be assembled from the existing principles that the platform offers. For instance, there is mostly no direct support of agent class as a feature of the agent platform, and agents are often treated as containers for objects representing behaviors (as in JADE.[9]). This means that a missing feature (agent class) is replaced by a concept (object as a container) existing in the language used (Java).

The guide could differ if it is intended for the current project only or if it should be used multiple times for various projects. In the first case, the methodology can be more specific and can omit the features that are not required by the particular conceptual model. Its development is then easier, faster and cheaper. If there is an assumption that it will be used repeatedly, the methodology should indeed cover all possibilities and contingencies of the model.

During the development of the transformation guide we can face the situation that the used platform cannot support the requirements of the conceptual model. We should not get into such a situation if we have made the selection of the platform carefully in the foregoing step, but if so, the choice of the platform has to be reconsidered.

Example

As an example we will transform the conceptual model into a platform-specific model in NetLogo.[10] NetLogo is a popular agent framework running on Logo. Logo is a structured language without true object-oriented features, hence the transformation of the conceptual model is not straightforward and it does not support some traits of agent-oriented programming that were discussed above (this is one reason why NetLogo was chosen for this example).

The following text stands for an example of a simplified transformation guide from the conceptual model to the platform-specific model for NetLogo. In the case of such simple models that can be created in NetLogo, they will be actually typically transformed directly from the conceptual diagram into the program code.

Agents   Given that Logo is a structured language, agents have to be transformed to data structures and code. Each agent is represented by a *breed* in Logo. Agent datastores are represented with *agent variables*. As data types are not distinguished in Logo, all

---

[9]See `http://jade.tilab.com` (visited on 12.12.2009)

datastores are de facto invariants. Because there are no true objects in NetLogo, all agent behaviors must be modeled as procedures that are called from a *go* procedure.

Association NetLogo contains *links* that can be used for modeling of associations. Links cannot bear any values, so in case it is inevitable, the value must be assigned to one of the participating agents.

Communication NetLogo does not support direct inter-agent communication. Communications must be therefore implemented as a part of behaviors' procedure code when the procedures directly adjust the values of agent variables.

Percepts Percepts of agents can be modeled as reading information from *patches*, agent variables of other agents or *globals*.

Actions Actions can be implemented as direct function calls or variable value adjustments of agents or of the environment (e.g., creating and disposing agents using *create* and *die* commands). The actions regarding spatial characteristics are represented mainly by dealing with *patches*.

Environment diagram Environment constructor can be modeled as a *setup* procedure in NetLogo. Other environment behaviors can be modeled as procedures called from a *go* procedure. Datastores of the environment should be modeled as *globals*.

Goals NetLogo has no support for goals, therefore agents must treat the goals through their behaviors.

Behaviors Code of each behavior described with an activity diagram should be transformed into a diagram of structured program. A good one for this purpose is the Jackson Structured Programming (JSP) diagram.[11,12]

Classes Logo does not support classes and other structured data types. The best option is to avoid them at all if possible. If necessary, they can be modeled as *breeds* and their association-relationships can be defined using *links*. However more sophisticated structures can be confusing and impractical and then it is better to reconsider using this platform.

User interface   There are two components of the user interface in NetLogo – the main screen and various gadgets for setting up of the simulation and observation of values produced. The conceptual model of the user interface should be transformed into the code in procedures that display agents and that back gadgets (*monitors, charts,* etc.) shown on the main dashboard. The values of environment options should be specified.

The process of transformation

a Describe the user interface.[13] Draw the structure of the surface (*patches*). Select the gadgets that will be used and assign them the respective *globals* and *reporters*.[14]

b Write down all agents into a table. Each agent should have specified its name in singular and plural (the name of the set in NetLogo) and a list of its variables.

c Define *globals* (datastores of environment).

d Define *links* for associations.

e Draw a JSP structure diagram of the *setup* procedure (i.e., the environment constructor)

f Create a list of all behaviors and draw a JSP structure diagram for each of them. Include handling of communications.

g Design procedures that serve the interface.

h Draw a JSP structure diagram of the *go* procedure.

This example demonstrates well the platform independence of the conceptual model in the sense of P3A.[15] If we had chosen any other platform, we can use it smoothly for the implementation of the same conceptual model just by rewriting this transformation guide.

8.2.7   Step 7 – Platform-specific model

Goal	to develop a specific, platform-dependent model on the selected platform from the conceptual model that was developed in the foregoing steps
Output	platform-depended model of the system
Participants	platform specialist

This step is optional and could be skipped in case the conceptual model will be transformed directly into the program code.

In this step, the transformation methodology developed in the foregoing section is applied on the conceptual model. Although it may seem that this step is just more or less a Cartesian product of the conceptual diagram and the transformation guide, the contrary is the case. Design of a platform-specific model is a creative process, because the platform specialist has to "bend" the elements of the conceptual model for the purposes of the platform-specific one, which is seldom straightforward. Some aspects that seem trouble-free in the conceptual model become very complicated when we need to apply them onto the particular platform and vice versa. The methodology developed in the foregoing step should lead the platform specialist the right way, but there are often still many challenges left that they have to solve. In the platform-specific model there can emerge new entities, data structures and other objects that were not contained in the conceptual model. On the other hand, some features that were specified in the conceptual diagram can be already implemented as the functions of the platform.

---

[10]See http://ccl.northwestern.edu/netlogo/docs (visited on 16.3.2010)

[11]Jackson 1975.

[12]Jackson Structured Programming was chosen deliberately to demonstrate that the methodology is compatible not only with the object-oriented, but also with the structured programming approach, although it is already used less frequently. For a closer description of how to read JSP diagrams see Appendix A.

[13]One can wonder why the user interface is the first thing to deal with. In NetLogo, the user interface is inseparably interconnected with the logic of the whole platform and hence it is a good departure point for the design of the system. Using different platforms, the user interface can be of much less importance.

[14]Reporter is the NetLogo equivalent of a function in other languages.

[15]Řepa 1999

Example

As an example of the platform-specific model, the following is a part of the simplified model of the intersection (from the previous chapters) for NetLogo developed on the basis of the guide from step 6. In this example, the platform-specific analysis looks much different than the conceptual analysis, because we use structured programming techniques. In most cases, using an object-oriented platform, the analysis on this level will have much in common with the conceptual model.

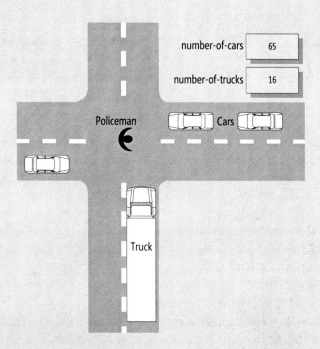

Figure 8.3 – A sketch of the user interface of the modeled simulation. Red captions are names of the respective entities – the agents and reporters backing monitors (dialog boxes containing the observed numbers of agents).

a) User interface   There are two kinds of agents that will be elaborated further in the following steps. There are two gadgets (monitors) that show numbers of the agents of the particular kind and therefore there are two reporters to be worked out that we add to the list of procedures. The suggested interface settings: unwrapped world, 128x128 patches.

Table 8.2 – An example of the list of reporters and procedures representing the elements of the user interface.

Procedure	Reporter	Comment
	number-of-cars	Return the number of cars that passed the intersection.
	number-of-trucks	Return the number of trucks that passed the intersection.

b) List of agents

Table 8.3 – An example of the list of agents for their development.

Agent	Agentset	Variables
Vehicle	Vehicles	xcor*, ycor*, heading*, speed, damage, color*
Policeman	Policemen	xcor*, ycor*, signal

The policeman's signal property will be used for the representation of communications. Because there is nothing like object inheritance in NetLogo, the type of vehicle (car or truck) is distinguished using the color variable. For practical purposes, the icon of the vehicle will be the same in both cases and the only visible difference will be its color (red for cars and blue for trucks).

For the values marked with an asterisk, the internal variables of NetLogo are used. Due to the absence of complex data structures in NetLogo and because it is more convenient, instead of holding a map object in memory, the agent will use data from the NetLogo environment (for example, position of agents).

c) **Define globals**   There are no globals. The notion about the traffic situation will be solved using inherent NetLogo variables – positions, directions and so on, of the agents in the simulation window.

d) **Define links for associations**   There are no associations in the simulation; that is, no links.

e) **Setup procedure**   The setup procedure (see Figure 8.4) simply creates one Policeman agent and one vehicle agent after the start of the simulation. The policeman will be put into the middle of the intersection and the vehicle will be put on the beginning of a random road. The vehicle will be of a random kind, with a random speed and direction.

f) Behaviors   The behaviors in Table 8.4 (among others[16]) should be implemented in the simulation.

Table 8.4 – An example of the list of reporters and procedures representing behaviors of agents and the environment.

Procedure	Reporter	Comment
traffic-observation		The related behavior can be handled by the inherent properties of the platform and does not require any special procedure.
damage-processing		Detection of collisions of vehicles. The procedure will calculate a level of damage and eventually dispose of the vehicle.
signal-reception		Communication with the Policeman will be simple (just reading of state variable of the agent) and therefore no special procedure is needed.
vehicle-control		Drive vehicle through the intersection. Traffic-observation functionalities are integrated in this procedure. For the JSP structure diagram of this procedure see Figure 8.5.
view-rendition		The related behavior can be handled by the inherent properties of the platform and does not require any special procedure.
collision-processing		Collisions can be treated on "agent side" in the damage-processing procedure. No "environment side" procedure.
move-processing		Movement of agents can be treated on the "agent side" in the damage-processing procedure. No "environment side" procedure.
...	...	

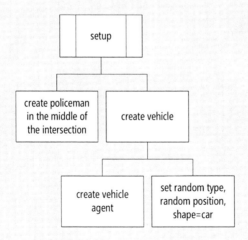

Figure 8.4 – JSP structure chart of `setup` function

As we can see, due to the specific features of the NetLogo platform, most of the agent and environment properties have shrunk into a few procedures.[17] Each remaining procedure and reporter should be elaborated individually. In Figure 8.5 there is an example of a JSP structure chart for the `vehicle-control` procedure. The procedure detects whether there is a vehicle ahead and if so, it starts breaking. The speed of the vehicle it decreased by 5 every simulation cycle until the car is fully stopped. The same will happen if the policeman signals to stop. Should no such a contingency happen, the vehicle will accelerate. Breaking action is detached into a separate procedure. In a real situation we would probably need a bit more sophisticated means of controlling of the vehicle.

g) Interface procedures   Both interface procedures (reporters) simply count the numbers of the individual kinds of vehicles and return them. There are no sophisticated algorithms that should be designed.

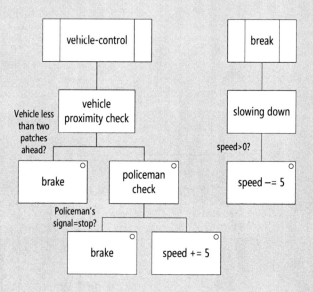

Figure 8.5 – JSP structure chart of the `vehicle-control` procedure.

h) Go procedure   The `go` procedure will continually call all the behaviors that were defined in the foregoing steps. First, for each vehicle, all its behaviors (vehicle-control, damage-processing, etc.) are called. Then the behaviors of the policeman agent are performed. Finally, if necessary, the procedures of the user interface would be called (not in this example).

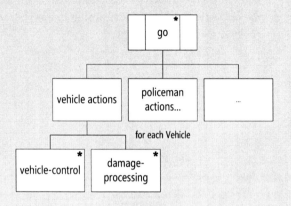

Figure 8.6 – JSP structure chart of go procedure

Summary   The overview of the simulation program structure is shown in Table 8.6 and Table 8.5.

Table 8.5 – A list of procedures and reporters of the model.

Procedure	Reporter	Diagram
	number-of-cars	N/A
	number-of-trucks	N/A
damage-processing		...
vehicle-control		Figure 8.5
...		...
setup		Figure 8.4
go		Figure 8.6

Table 8.6 – A list of agents of the model.

Agent	Agentset	Variables
Vehicle	Vehicles	xcor, ycor, heading, speed, damage, color
Policeman	Policemen	xcor, ycor, signal

8.2.8   Step 8 – Development, debugging and testing

Goal	to develop a program code of an agent-based simulation on the platform selected in step 6 according to the platform-specific model from step 7
Output	the program code of the simulation
Participants	programmer, tester

In this step, the simulation is developed using the methods common in the selected platform. There is no substantial difference in the mere coding between a multi-agent system and any other kind of software.

Special attention should be devoted to debugging and testing of multi-agent systems (and hence agent-based simulations). Simpler systems can be more or less successfully tested using the usual methods. Unfortunately, in the case of bigger and more complex simulations, testing in the conventional way becomes very inconvenient. Multi-agent systems are composed of the individual agents that are separately testable in the traditional way. In addition, however, an integral part of multi-agent systems are the mutual relationships of these agents, their relationships with the agent environment, and incidental emergent properties that appear in the system. Simply said, we cannot deem a multi-agent system just a sum of its parts. The emergent properties of the entire system are even more important than in a "traditional" information system, so a different approach to testing is needed.

The main idea of testing agent-based simulations proposed in this methodology is to divide the testing of a multi-agent system into three "layers."[18] In the first layer we conduct unit testing of the individual agents. We test whether functionality of the agents corresponds with their design objectives. In the second layer, the testing of agent interactions is performed. We search there for the errors coming from the agent interactions, because even if the individual agent is working properly, hidden errors could still show up during the interaction of two or more agents. The third layer constitutes testing of the entire multi-agent system. Although we may find the individual agents as well as their interactions errorless, the whole system could still fail. On this level, performance

---

[16]The list is not complete as we have not elaborated other components of the system, for example Policeman agent.
[17]In many other cases, the situation can be inverse.
[18]Šalamon 2009.

problems and bottlenecks of system hubs, and vulnerability to mass collapses of agents could appear.

On the first layer we test the individual agents using a so-called *Mock Agent*. Mock Agent is a dummy agent without inner functionality. It possesses a proper interface to communicate with the tested agent. Mock Agent can send and receive messages to and from the tested agent and a programmer can evaluate whether the reaction of the tested agent is correct. During testing we can observe the internal states of the tested agent using tools like agent inspector, logging and others if they are present in the agent framework. Mock agents are good tools for testing inter-agent relationships, but they are less convenient for testing agent interaction with the environment; that is, testing percepts and actions of the agent. If we need to test, for example, vehicles in the simulated intersection, their mutual communication is not enough to evaluate the whole simulation. Testing of the agent should be conducted in the "production" environment if possible. If we have no such environment, it is necessary to build at least a small part of it for testing purposes (let's say, an intersection and its surroundings, in our example) and include it into the test suite. We call such a piece of environment a *stage*. The stage is an additional part of the test suite. As an example of a stage, we can use a traffic simulation, where agents are the cars and the stage is a part of a "map." It is not meaningful to test traffic simulation just with cars "hung" in space, so we need a stage to put them in. The stage could be quite complex, as in the case of the traffic simulation, or somewhat simple, as a numeric value on an agent's sensor function.

On the second layer, agent interactions are tested. A multi-agent system is not just an aggregate of its parts; it possesses emergent properties too, which begin to appear as soon as two or more agents begin to interoperate. For this reason, failures could show up even in a system with 100% error-free agents. Typical examples of errors of this kind are deadlocks, livelocks and various other kinds of conflicts. Detection of deadlocks is generally an issue in distributed systems. In running an agent-based situation with hundreds or thousands of agents, this can be a challenging task. One of the possible ways is a relatively simple stochastic approach based on the observation of agent messaging. Every executed interaction (especially actions and communications) in the running system is logged down into a table (a source agent, a destination agent and a kind of the interaction). Each logged interaction has a score. When the interaction occurs, we examine the table to see whether there is already such an interaction recorded. If so, we increase its score by a certain value (let's say 2); otherwise we add it into the table. After every simulation round, we decrease the score of each agent in the table by 1. The interactions with the highest (and growing) scores are candidates for deadlocks.

The third layer is focused on the system as a whole. For purposes of development of agent-based simulations on an existing working agent platform the relevant problem is unveiling system bottlenecks. Although multi-agent systems belong to distributed systems, there are often some central points (such as messaging services) in the system

that can turn out into bottlenecks. Testing of the multi-agent system on the third layer
should be focused mainly on measuring the performance of the system. The duration
of one simulation round, its variance through time, the speed of message delivery, the
length of message queues and so on, could be used as metrics.

Example

The following is a part of the code developed from the platform-specific model from
the previous steps. There are defined breeds representing agents, their datastores,
user-interface reporters and a part of the setup procedure.

> **Listing** – Part of the code of the agent-based simulation developed according to the
> platform-specific analysis from step 7. (NetLogo)

```
breed [vehicles vehicle]
breed [policemen policeman]

vehicles-own [speed, damage]
policemen-own [signal]

to-report number-of-cars
  report count vehicles with [color = red]
end

to-report number-of-trucks
  report count vehicles with [color = blue]
end

to setup
  create-policemen 1
  ...
```

8.2.9   Step 9 – Model evaluation

Goal	to test the developed model for its plausibility and its conformance with the modeled reality
Output	finished model
Participants	tester, expert

In this moment, we have working software – the agent-based simulation. It is debugged and tested, so it works as expected and provides us with output data. The development process of an ordinary software application would be finished here, but in the case of the agent-based model, the mere function of the system is not enough, because the conformance with reality is required. Even if the system is working properly, it may generate misleading and/or useless data. This step in the development process should assess the output.

The principle of this step is merely to check the model if it behaves as expected. It is not easy to say generally how the testing should be performed, because it depends heavily on the character of the simulation. In the case of economic simulations, we often have a time series of values of certain indicators. Testing of the model can be performed by comparison of the values generated by the model with real situation data. If the generated data conforms with real data, the model is probably all right. The match between generated and real data is never perfect; in fact we do not compare the values, but trends and the whole dynamics. In other cases, where there is no time series or other "hard data" (as in the case of traffic simulations), criteria stemming from the particular situation should be derived.

Testers perform the evaluation of the model. They test it according to the criteria stated by experts that should be included in the very first step of the development process: the task formulation. Because the project often shifts and evolves during its development, the criteria should be reviewed and eventually updated. The expert's task is to recognize if the model fits well enough the purpose it was built for.

8.3   Agent Conceptual Modeling

In this part, diagrams and principles for agent conceptual modeling are introduced. Design of multi-agent systems and agent-based simulation brings certain requirements that cannot be fulfilled by present modeling languages. In this chapter a modeling language for agent-based simulations is proposed. The language is primarily intended to be used with Agentology, but it can be applied independently as well.

Software modeling is a highly developed field, where many questions have been already solved. Due to that fact, there is no point to try devising everything from scratch. A completely new set of diagrams and methods could hardly be better than methodologies that are being developed and continually improved for years, and the need to train specialists would make using a completely new methodology extremely costly. The aim was to use as much as possible from the existing modeling languages and methodologies and to develop just what is still missing or markedly unsatisfactory in agent modeling. Due to that fact, some existing diagrams from UML (which is often deemed a de facto modeling standard) are used just with minor changes for agent modeling. The other diagrams that were developed from the beginning follow usual rules and conventions, so learning them is easy. All diagrams, including new ones, can be constructed using elements and artifacts from UML, so they can be created in any UML-compatible CASE tool. Knowledge of UML (at least on a basic level) is required for using this methodology, because it is considered superfluous to describe again what is already written in OMG standards.[19]

Although the conceptual model does not support any particular technology, it is based on the general principles of agent-oriented programming as defined in chapter 5. It is perhaps convenient to recall that agent-oriented programming is considered a next level of abstraction in programming and so everything "inside" agents is deemed an object (analogous to object-oriented programming, where the content of the objects comes from the structured world).

This means all behaviors, datastores and even interactions of agents are objects. It can seem contradictory to the previous statement about platform independence of the conceptual model, but there is no inconsistency. Object is a very expedient abstraction that can wrap almost anything from simple primitive types to complex data structures or stores of logical facts. This is a handy principle for the comprehension of the agent model, and it is no problem that there finally does not need to be any object at all in the specific implementation.

There are two layers of the conceptual model. The higher layer (agent diagrams) treats the whole agents as indivisible units. It is oriented toward entities and their relationships. It consists of agent diagrams, goal diagrams and environment diagrams. They are typically developed first and constitute a declaratory level of the conceptual model that describes the structure of the system, its parts and the relationships among them. It describes how the parts act, not how exactly the parts work inside.

The lower layer (particle diagrams) concerns the insides of agents and is more process-oriented. As atoms are composed of elementary particles, agent diagrams are composed of the particle diagrams that describe the internal aspects of agents. There are *class diagrams, communication diagrams* and *activity diagrams* among particle diagrams. They follow up and develop the content of agent diagrams. Particle diagrams are mostly derived from UML diagrams and use a similar syntax that should make training easier.

8.3.1   Agent Diagrams

An *agent diagram* can be used on two basic levels of granularity. On a *global* level, they should encompass the whole system. They describe all kinds of agents in the multi-agent system, their relationships, the interactions with the environment and the interactions with each other. On a *detailed* level, agent diagrams focus on the individual agents and their features. A *goal diagram* is used for the representation of complex goals of agents.

---

[19]*OMG Unified Modeling LanguageTM (OMG UML), Superstructure* 2009.

An *environment diagram* describes the services of the environment and its communication with the agents.

Global level

On the global level agent diagram consists of agents (agent classes) and all kinds of their relationships.

The agents should be drawn as rectangles with the name of the agent and eventually with a certain stereotype if needed. After or under the agent's name, there should be written an agent's goal in brackets (see Figure 8.7a). Goals are of such a high importance in the agent world that they should be treated from the very beginning of the design process. In a majority of cases one goal is enough for most agents. Sometimes, however, the situation is more complicated, and multiple goals or changes in goals are needed. In that case we put an asterisk into the brackets (see Figure 8.7b) and the agent's goals will be specified in a specific goal diagram (see section 8.3.1).

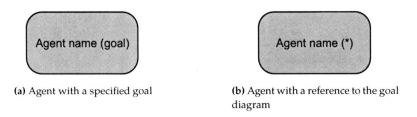

(a) Agent with a specified goal   (b) Agent with a reference to the goal diagram

Figure 8.7 – Agent artifacts in agent diagram

Agents are interconnected with the environment and with each other through their relationships. According to the model of the agent's communication (see section 3.2 on page 23), the agent senses the percepts from the environment and takes actions that influence it. Besides that, the environment and other agents can apply various actions on it. Moreover, the agents communicate with each other.

There can be three kinds of interaction in the global agent diagrams:

- *Communication* (see Figure 8.8) between two or more agents is instant, one-shot interaction. It starts, comes through and ends in a certain, very limited period of time. Communication can be relatively complicated and then it has to be elaborated in a separate kind of diagram (see chapter 8.3.2). Communication is not an object, but a sequence of objects (messages); therefore it cannot bear a value per se. It is voluntary for both sides. No agent is obliged to step into such interaction and each side can cancel the interaction at any time (the concrete situation depends on the negotiation protocol). Communication is depicted with a dashed line.

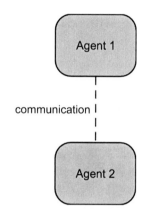

Figure 8.8 – Communication

(a) An action of the environment on agent and an action of the agent
on the environment

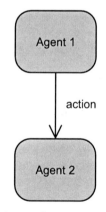

(b) Action of an agent on another
agent

Figure 8.9 – Actions

- *Action* (see Figure 8.9) is a one-way and one-shot interaction when the environment influences one agent or an agent willingly influences another one or the environment. Unlike the aforementioned interaction, it is voluntary just for one side – the originator of the relation, but it is obligatory for the other one. Agent action on another agent is relatively rare in comparison with the actions of the environment, and it is often of a negative nature (killing or damaging of other agents), but it may not be always true (agents can for example create other agents). The environment can always create and dispose of an agent; however, these two kinds of action are not necessary to draw as they are considered implicit. Agent action is depicted with a solid simple arrow between two agents. Action of the environment is depicted with black dots and a simple arrow with solid line to the agent's rectangles.

- *Percepts* (see Figure 8.10) are information from the environment that represent an agent's sensory input. For example, a car agent perceives the situation on the road. For the agent it is voluntary information – it is not obliged to react, but the environment has to provide it. In Agentology, the percepts are depicted as black dots with the simple arrow with a dashed line to the agent's rectangles.

Figure 8.10 – Percept and agent's action on the environment

An interaction line or arrow of any kind except the actions between an agent and the environment and percepts can also start and end in the rectangle of the same agent. This means that there can be an interaction between the agents of the same type (class).

An agent can have the same interaction with other agents *simultaneously*. This means, there is a simultaneous communication of more participants; that is, a one-to-many relationship (e.g., an auction) or even a many-to-many relationship. Then it is possible to depict it as a multiplicity with the same notation as in the case of UML class diagrams.

A modeler can often have a problem distinguishing, which interaction should be modeled as a communication with another agent and what is the percept from the environment or an action. A typical example could be, for instance, a detection of another agent in a room. If one agent tries to discover if it has another one ahead, should it be modeled as a communication with the second agent or as a percept? The right answer stems from the fact that unlike the case of an object method, the agent's action cannot be guaranteed. It is solely up to the agent's will, whether it will react or not. However, percepts are guaranteed by the environment. If one agent can simply see another one, then it should be modeled as a percept, because the environment will always provide true information about the position of the other agents regardless of their will. But if the agents, for example, talked on radio, the detection of the other agent would depend on their will to participate or not. And in that case, it should be modeled as a communication.

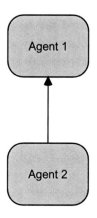

Figure 8.11 – Generalization–specialization relationship

Thus, the rule of thumb is as follows. If the fact whether the agent gets the information depends on the will of another agent, then it is inter-agent interaction. If it is information that the agent should always surely acquire, then it should be modeled as a percept.

Modeling of interactions is a novel feature in agent-oriented programming which has no direct counterpart in object-oriented programming. Otherwise there are the same kinds of relationships that can be defined between objects. Particularly there is a *generalization-specialization* relationship and an *association* relationship.

- Agents can inherit some features from their antecedents and add others in the next generation (*generalization-specialization* relationship, see Figure 8.11). An example is a general vehicle-agent and its car and truck child-agents. Agent classes can be declared abstract (using stereotype) as well, if it arises from context. If we are not sure if we should displace common features of more agents into the general one, we can draw them separately and leave the decision for later consideration on a detailed level. The symbol of generalization-specialization relationship is an arrow with a filled arrow.

- *Association* (see Figure 8.12) between two or more agents is a relationship that lasts longer than communication, for a significant amount of time or even for the entire run of the simulation. It can be typically contracts, liabilities or obligations

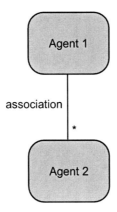

Figure 8.12 – Association relationship

or other kinds of liaisons between the agents. The association can bear a value (e.g., the relationship between agent employee and agent employer with wage as a parameter). Association is voluntary for both sides and is depicted with a solid line.

Example

In the following picture there is an agent diagram on a global level of an intersection that is controlled by a policeman who assigns priority to vehicles on the roads. There are vehicles that can be either cars or trucks (but there cannot be mere vehicle-agents, because the agent class is abstract). Their goals are more complex and are depicted with a goal diagram. Note that the special agent classes (Truck and Car) inherit the goals from the abstract class. They are able to observe the traffic situation and move accordingly. There is a policeman that observes the intersection, controls traffic and signals to vehicles. They may or may not obey them. The goal of the policeman agent is to keep traffic smooth. Vehicles can cause a car crash, but they cannot, for example, run over the policeman.

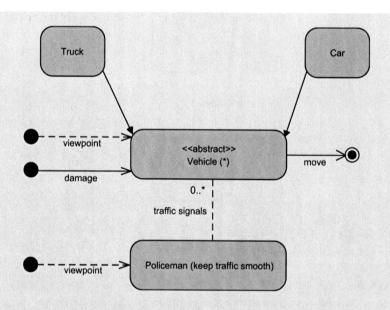

Figure 8.13 – Conceptual model of an intersection

The second example is from another field and it demonstrates actions and inheritance. There are owners of bank accounts. Some of the account owners are bailiffs that foreclose money of defaulters (i.e., a bailiff is a special kind of account owner). Any account owner can send funds to another account owner (and it is credited to his or her account). Only bailiffs can collect money from the accounts of account owners without their consent.

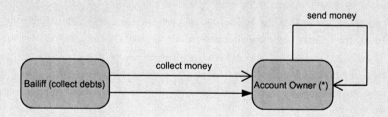

Figure 8.14 – Conceptual model – sending and receiving money

Detailed level

We can say that the agent diagram on a detailed level (Figure 8.15) provides the same picture as its global counterpart, but with a higher "zoom." Unlike the global diagram that describes the whole system, the detailed level covers the individual agents and describes their internal constitution.

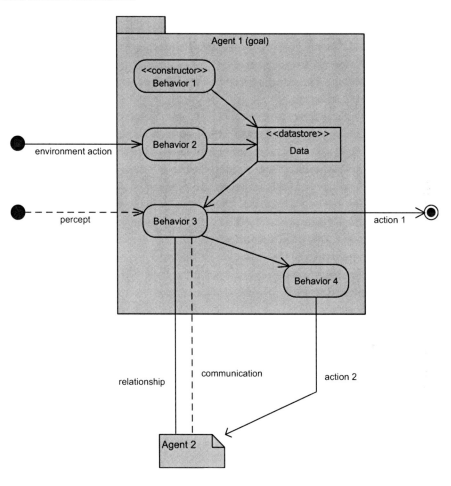

Figure 8.15 – Agent Diagram (detailed level)

In each of them, the agent is depicted with a big rectangle that represents the boundary between inside and outside of the agent. On the top of the rectangle there is a caption with the name of the agent and its goal (the same rules as on the global level). There are also sketched all the relationship lines and arrows from and to the agent that are drawn in the global diagram.

As described in chapter 5, agents consist of behaviors, data and goals, where behaviors are the agent's operations (just as methods are the operations of objects) that persist over time, and the agent has total control over their running.

Behaviors are depicted as rectangles inside the agent. There can be two special kinds of behaviors: constructor behavior and destructor behavior. Analogous to the object world, constructor behavior (*constructor* stereotype) is launched at the beginning of the agent's life, and destructor behavior (*destructor* stereotype) is launched right before the agent is disposed of. The purpose of the constructor is to set up the initial state of a newly created agent instance and the purpose of the destructor is to perform eventual closing and cleaning operations. Because the action that creates the agent is implicit, there is no need to show it in the diagram.

Besides behaviors, an agent contains data. Data are represented by datastores. Data can be written to the datastores and read from them solely by behaviors. Due to a strict encapsulation of agents, there is no access to their data except through behaviors. This means a datastore is like a sink. There must be a faucet and there must be a drain. Datastores must be interconnected with behaviors and behaviors with each other by simple arrows representing events / data flows. There can be a confusion that stems from the fact that the resultant diagram resembles an activity diagram to some extent, but this is a false impression. A detailed agent diagram does not contain any sequence of actions, because the behaviors last by definition for the life of the agent and they can only change their resultant conduct depending upon input data. The principle of the representation of the internal structure of a detailed agent diagram is much like the principle of a data-flow diagram.

Example

In the following figure there is an elaboration of an agent diagram on a detailed level of the abstract Vehicle agent from the global agent diagram in Figure 8.13.

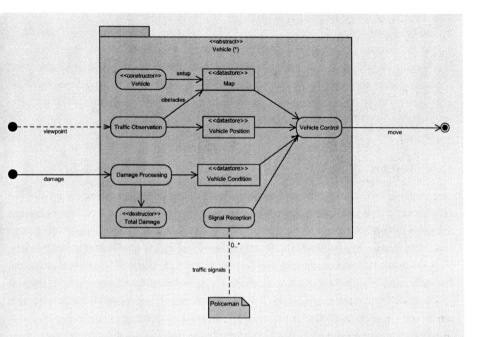

Figure 8.16 – An example of agent diagram (detailed level)

The diagram can be read as follows: after the creation of the agent, a map is set up in memory. The agent monitors the situation ahead with Traffic Observation behavior and stores information into Vehicle Position (coordinates) and Map (obstacles, that is the objects ahead of the vehicle) datastores. The information about the traffic situation is a percept, which means that the agent may or may not take it into consideration. A different situation is a damage action that can be applied to the agent by the environment in the case of, for example, a crash of the vehicle. This must be processed by Damage Processing behavior. The result can be either written into the Vehicle Condition datastore or – in the case of total destruction of the vehicle – Total Damage behavior must be called. Total Damage is a destructor behavior that causes all behaviors to stop and dispose of the agent. There is another behavior called Signal Reception that communicates with the Policeman agent; the communication is unidirectional (from Policeman to Vehicle), but it is not yet apparent from this diagram. The last behavior of the agent is Vehicle Control, which makes decisions about the direction and pace of agent motion using the information from all mentioned datastores and the information about signals provided by Signal Reception behavior.

Why is all information except traffic signals stored into a datastore, but the signals are provided directly by the behavior? The information about vehicle position, obstacles on the road and its condition become a part of the agent's knowledge and it should be stored for future use (it can be indeed also updated by more recent information before it is used). Sometimes the distinction between these two ways may not be so clear. But the information about traffic signals on the specific intersection has little if any value for any future use, so it is not necessary to store it and the agent can always work with the immediate value provided by the behavior.

Goal diagram

A goal diagram is a diagram on the global level of the analysis and serves for the description of agent goals, especially when an agent has multiple goals, when it changes the goals during the operation or in other advanced cases. If the agent has just one goal (a usual situation), the goal diagram can be replaced just by the goal statement in brackets of agent artifacts in the agent diagram (see section 8.3.1). The goal diagram stems from the state machine diagram of UML. Each goal is represented by a rectangle with the text of the goal. Optionally there can be a priority of the goal, expressed, for example, by a numerical value in brackets. This is useful if there are conflicting goals. To avoid confusion with the activity diagram, it is recommended to draw the goal diagram's rectangles with dashed lines. In Figure 8.17 there is a structure of a goal diagram with one goal. Such a diagram would have exactly the same meaning as the goal written in brackets in the agent diagram.

Figure 8.17 – The structure of goal diagram

An arrow from one goal to another means changing goals. Normally the goal is changed when the earlier one is reached or abandoned. The arrow can contain a condition of goal change if needed. See Figure 8.18.

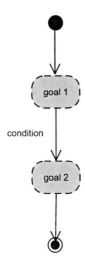

Figure 8.18 – One goal is reached or abandoned and changed for another

Agents sometimes have more concurrent goals in the same moment. If we need to express it with a goal diagram, we can use a fork and join elements from the state machine diagram (see Figure 8.19).

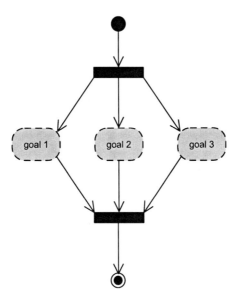

Figure 8.19 – Multiple simultaneous goals

In some cases the selection of further goals depends on certain criteria. For that purpose it is possible to draw a selection of goals depending on a condition (see Figure 8.20).

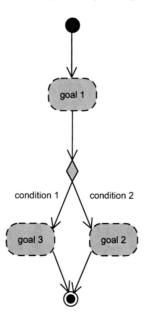

Figure 8.20 – Conditional goals

Goal diagrams look like activity diagrams or state machine diagrams but they should be never confused. First, a goal diagram is a diagram on a general, global level of granularity, whereas activity diagrams describe internal processes of the behaviors of the individual agents. Second, activity diagrams depict actions that the agent's behavior performs along with the respective agent states, while the goal diagram's purpose is to describe states that the agent strives to reach. And finally, goals are relatively complex and "robust." Unlike actions, they do not describe the individual steps of a certain process, but they represent an objective that should be reached by a chain of particular actions. This means that goal diagrams are often much simpler than typical activity diagrams.

Example

In the following picture there is an example of a goal diagram of a vehicle agent. The first goal of the agent is to *obtain the destination* of its route. After this goal is reached, there are two simultaneous goals: *get to the destination* and *avoid crash*. Because *avoid crash* has a higher priority, the second goal could be suppressed if there was a risk of a crash. If the agent gets to the destination on time, it obtains a new destination and the whole situation repeats. If it is too late, its new goal is to *get back*. Because there is no priority value on the *get back* goal, it is considered it to have the same priority as its predecessor.

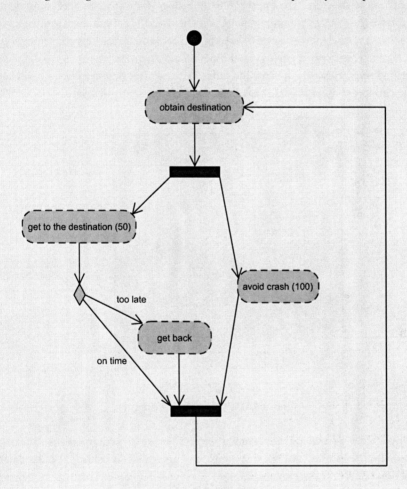

Figure 8.21 – Example of goal diagram

Environment diagram

Environment[20] is often omitted by most of the other agent methodologies, but it has so crucial an impact on every agent-based simulation that it should be considered in the conceptual model. The problem of environment is that it is a ubiquitous matter that is hard to describe. The approach to modeling of the environment in Agentology stems from the fact that from the agents' point of view, the environment is often nothing more than a special kind of agent-like entity that communicates with other agents in the simulation. Therefore an environment diagram closely resembles an agent diagram on a detailed level. However, it is not the same, because after all, the rules for modeling of the environment differ in some characteristics from modeling of agents.

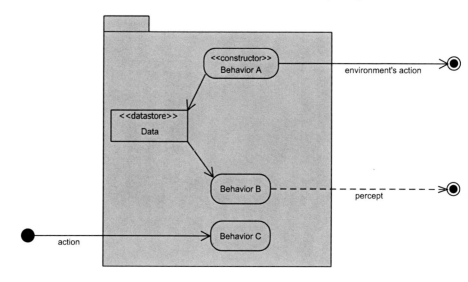

Figure 8.22 – Environment diagram

There is a big rectangle that contains what is "inside" the environment – that is, behaviors and datastores. All the rest – meaning agents – is outside.[21] Unlike detailed agent diagrams, the environment diagram has no header name. There can be behaviors (including constructor and destructors) and datastores in the environment. No environment behavior can communicate or be a party in association or in a generalization-specialization relationship. Only actions and percepts are allowed. Unlike the case of agents, percepts are placed in the output of the environment.

---

[20] For more on agent environments see chapter 3.1.

[21] It could sound a little bit confusing, because agents are considered being "inside" the environment. However, in this meaning "inside" stands for the service routines that together create the environment.

Example

In the following figure there is an elaboration of an environment diagram for the model depicted in the global agent diagram in Figure 8.13. The situation is rather simple. There is a constructor that sets up the simulation, which means the creation of all agents and writing their current positions into the Traffic Situation datastore. This datastore contains the map of the situation and positions and directions of all agents. View Rendition behavior provides viewpoint percepts for the Vehicles and the Policeman (note that there is just one environment for all agents). This means that it renders current traffic situation information for every single agent from its individual point of view and sends it to the agent that asked.

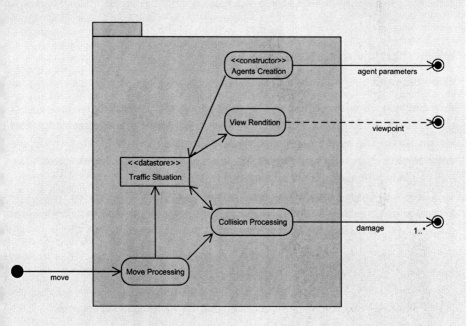

Figure 8.23 – An example of environment diagram

No agent gets the big picture, but just the part of the situation that it could see. Data like positions, directions and speeds of other vehicles, shape of the road, etc. are provided. View Rendition taps data from Traffic Situation datastore. If there is a collision, it proceeds to the Collision Processing behavior which handles it, calculates damage of vehicles and sends it as an action to the vehicles. Note that there is a multiplicity mark at the damage-action. This is because damage caused by one agent can affect more of them, so the action can be applied simultaneously to one or more agents.

One can say it is inconsistent to hold information about positions of agents twice: first in the environment's Traffic Situation and second in the Vehicle-agent's Vehicle Position datastores. In the object-oriented world this would be true, but it is not the case with agents. Information that is contained in objects is sure and objects have to give it to anyone who asks through calling their methods. The agent paradigm typically works with the assumption that information contained in the agent is just a belief (the agent believes that it is true, but cannot be sure, because it has no access to "impersonal truth"). This is a useful supposition particularly in agent-based models, because it is exactly how the real world works. The entire situation is stored only in the environment's Traffic Situation datastore, but no agent (in contrast to the researcher) has a direct access to it, so it depends solely on the percepts that it gets from the environment. Note that there is a duplicate representation of the traffic situation.

8.3.2   Particle diagrams

Class diagram

As mentioned above, everything inside agents are objects, particularly the messages of interactions and datastores. For objects we already have enough modeling instruments we can apply. The most important is the class diagram from UML[22] that we can use without much change for modeling of datastores and interactions between agents (except communication, which will be discussed further).

Class diagrams are modeled as usual, according to the UML reference. While creating class diagrams, the modeler sometimes discovers problems and mistakes in agent diagrams. In that case, agent diagrams should be indeed corrected.

Example

In the following picture, there are class diagrams of Vehicle-agent's datastores.

---

[22]*OMG Unified Modeling LanguageTM (OMG UML), Superstructure* 2009.

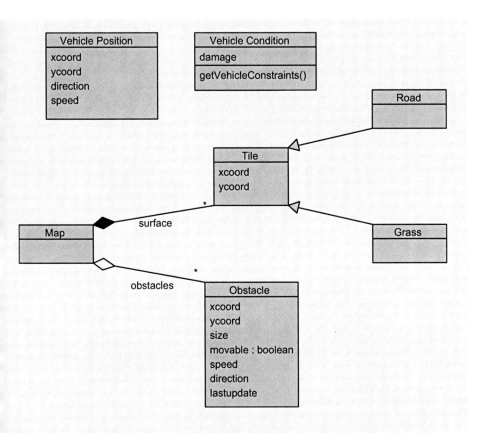

Figure 8.24 – Class diagrams of agent's datastores

There are three datastores. For the Vehicle Position datastore, there is a simple class, where coordinates, speed and direction of the agent should be stored. For vehicle condition, there is another simple class, where information about damage of the vehicle should be stored. There is set no data type for damage, which means it is completely up to those who will implement the model. Damage can be stored in a certain data structure, in numeric values representing the degree of impairment or in logic facts, and so on. If the modeler had special requirements, he or she could indicate them into a textual comment.

The last datastore – the Map – is a little bit more complex. It consists of the representation of surface that is composed of "tiles," the building blocks that can either represent road or grass. Both contain coordinates. Besides the surface, the map contains also information about the obstacles that the agent can see around. There are coordinates, size, speed and direction of each object, information about the last update of the information about the obstacle (the older the information, the lower the value it has). There is also a movable attribute (exceptionally with Boolean type) that can seem redundant, because there is already an attribute with data about the vehicle's speed. However, movable contains the information about the object's general ability to move, but speed contains data about its immediate pace. Even if speed could be zero in the moment, it does not mean the object cannot move at all and that the object must be there in the future. But if movable is true, the agent can be sure that the object will stay on the spot.

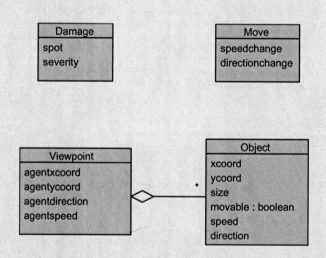

Figure 8.25 – Class diagrams of agent's interactions

There are class diagrams in Figure 8.25 that represent classes of agent references.

Damage contains information about damage suffered. Using the Move action the agent sends requirements for changes in its speed and direction. On the other hand, using Viewpoint the environment returns information about the agent's immediate position, speed and direction. Note that the agent's Move action represents its endeavor – for example, to stop – but using Viewpoint, the environment returns a true result, which may or may not be in conformance with the agent's wish. Besides information about the agent's actual position and velocity, information about objects around the agent is provided. They can be later transformed into data that will be stored in Map datastores (obstacles).

Communication diagram

Communication is typically much more complex than other kinds of agent interaction. It represents negotiation between two or more agents. As discussed theoretically in chapter 4, agent communication is never incidental. It must be performed according to a communication protocol. Communication diagrams then simply denote a graphical representation of such communication protocols.

Communication diagrams stem from Sequence Diagrams from UML.[23] Because sequence diagrams describe dynamics between objects in an object-oriented system, particularly the sequences of method calls, but the purpose of communication diagrams is to describe one kind of interaction between agents that is much different in principle, the name of the diagram was changed to avoid confusion. Generally we can say that if not stated otherwise, communication diagrams should be constructed according to the same rules as UML sequence diagrams.

For every single communication that is depicted in agent diagrams, there should be a communication diagram. A communication diagram is a rectangle. The keyword *cd* followed by the name of communication (identical to the name of the communication in the agent diagram) is in a "snipped-corner" pentagon in the upper-left corner of the rectangle.

The communication diagram shows agents (usually two, but there can be more of them) participating in the communication and the individual messages arranged in a time sequence. Each participating agent has a so-called lifeline. Messages in sequence diagrams are ordered according to a time axis from top to bottom. Messages are represented by arrows between lifelines. There should be a class diagram for each message that specifies the data structure of the message. Unlike sequence diagrams, there can only be regular lifeline participants representing agents (no actors, system boundaries, etc.). Agents can have assigned a multiplicity (as usual in class diagrams). This means that an agent of one kind communicates with a certain number of agents of another kind simultaneously. This is a relatively common situation in agent modeling. In Figure 8.26, one instance of Agent 1 communicates with one or more instances of Agent 2 concurrently.

The main difference between sequence and communication diagrams is in treating of messages. In the object-oriented world, sending messages (method calls) is mostly synchronous, which causes a de facto hierarchical arrangement of sequence diagrams. Most called methods are pending until it finishes all its code and then returns a value (albeit sometimes void). If such method calls another method, it must wait until the called method finishes all its duties including, for example, calling another methods. This means that the LIFO principle is applied and the first called method terminates as the last. There are indeed asynchronous calls possible as well, but they are much less common in object-oriented programming.

In the agent world, a natural way of sending messages is asynchronous (see chapter 5.3). An agent does not stop and wait after calling another agent. The called agent need not return a value. There is no certainty that the called agent will reply at all. The result is that the communication diagram is much less hierarchical.

---

[23]*OMG Unified Modeling LanguageTM (OMG UML), Superstructure* 2009.

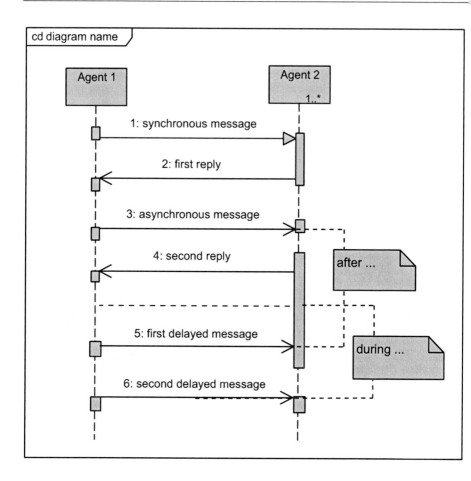

Figure 8.26 – Communication diagram

There can be still two kinds of messages sent between agents: synchronous and asynchronous. Asynchronous messages are depicted with a stick arrowhead and they mean that the agent does not wait until it receives a reply but continues immediately with other operations. Synchronous messages are depicted with a solid arrowhead and they mean that the agent waits for a reply or that reply is required. There are no dotted return messages as in sequence diagrams due to the fact that there are no return values in agents. In Figure 8.26 examples of synchronous and asynchronous messages are shown.

Another difference is in the meaning of the thin rectangle drawn along the lifeline. In sequence diagrams this means the activation of the object or the duration between calling a method and receiving a return value. Because agents are activated permanently, this symbol is used differently in the communication diagram. First, it means an interval

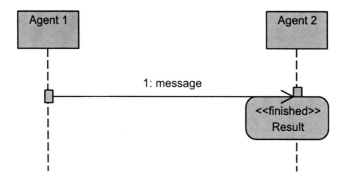

Figure 8.27 – Marking a state of communication

when a certain message can be sent. In Figure 8.26, message 4 can be sent not only after message 3, but also after message 5. This is particularly useful in more complex protocols with conditions and iterations. Second, in the case of synchronous messages, when used on a destination lifeline it joins request-messages with its answers. In Figure 8.26 messages 1 and 2 are joined, because message 1 is synchronous.

Sometimes, messages have to be constrained. The most common case involves time constrains where there is a certain time-out during or after which the message should be sent. The constraint is denoted by a note on the side of diagram and by a dashed line that shows the beginning and the end of the constraint. In Figure 8.26 message 5 can be sent no sooner than after a certain time after message 3. Sometimes we need not only a delay given to a particular message but given to a larger block of messages that should be finished. This can be depicted with a dashed line. Message 6 in Figure 8.26 should be sent during a certain time period after at least messages 1-4 are sent (these can include also message 5).

In agent communication it is quite often necessary to mark a certain state of the communication process. It is possible to do so by means of a rectangle at certain place on the agent's lifeline. In Figure 8.27 there is a mark at the end of communication. For such a purpose it is handy to use the «finished» stereotype.

A communication protocol is a kind of a structured program. Any structured program could be expressed using a combination of sequence, selection and iteration.[24] A sequence is a series of messages that were discussed above. The instruments for representation of selections and iterations are taken from the UML 2 sequence diagram and they are depicted in Figures 8.28 and 8.29.

The last component of communication diagrams is a reference that represents "subprogram calls" in structured programming. This means that the diagram references an-

---

[24]Dahl, Dijkstra, and Hoare 1972.

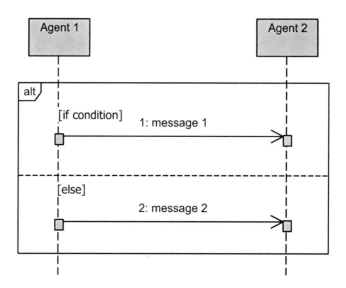

Figure 8.28 – Selection in communication diagram

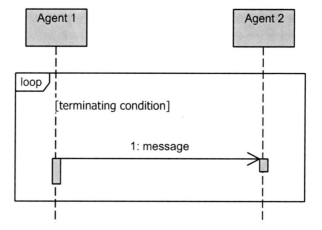

Figure 8.29 – Iteration in communication diagram

other diagram rather than defining a certain part of the communication process. References were also fully adopted from the UML 2 sequence diagram and the scheme of their usage is shown in Figure 8.30.

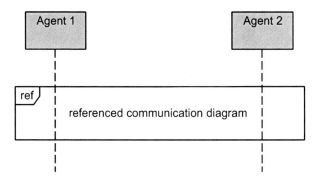

Figure 8.30 – References in communication diagram

Example

As an example of a communication diagram there is a scheme of a classical English auction in Figure 8.31. There are two kinds of agents in the relationship: Auctioneer and Bidder. There can be one or more bidders (1..* multiplicity), but just one auctioneer. The auctioneer opens the auction and awaits bids. If no bid is placed within 60 seconds, the auction is canceled.

If a bid is placed (message 2), it must be confirmed or rejected. The auctioneer confirms the bid if it is equal or higher that the standing bid plus a minimum step. This is repeated over and over as long as new bids come. If there is no new bid even after 30 seconds, the auctioneer-agent sends the signal "going" (message 5) which is repeated if there is no new bid for another 30 seconds. Finally, if there is no new bid even after another 30 seconds from message 5, auctioneer sends the signal "gone" (message 6) and the communication protocol is over.

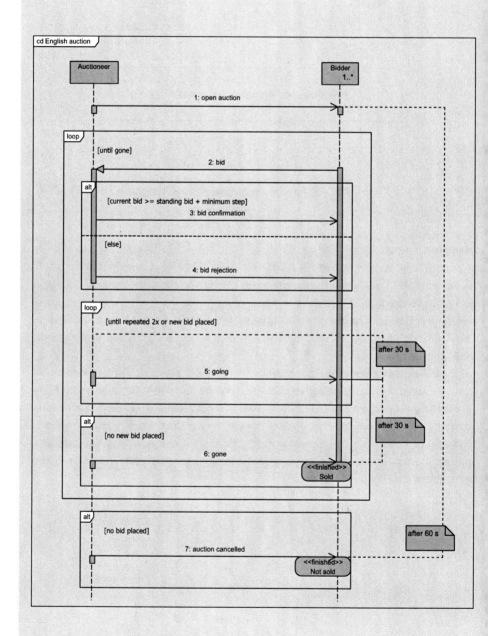

Figure 8.31 – An example of communication diagram

Activity diagram

Activity diagrams are popular diagrams from UML that are used for modeling a system's dynamics. In the agent-world, activity diagrams are especially suitable for detailed modeling of behaviors (agent's operations). The rules for using activity diagrams in agent conceptual modeling are basically the same as in the case of traditional UML. In UML, one activity diagram typically means one system process. In the agent world, one activity diagram usually means one behavior.

The only substantial difference between traditional UML activity diagrams and agent activity diagrams is their integration with other diagrams of the agent conceptual model. Given that activity diagrams represent behavior of an agent, they have to cope with all kinds of interactions the agent can participate in.

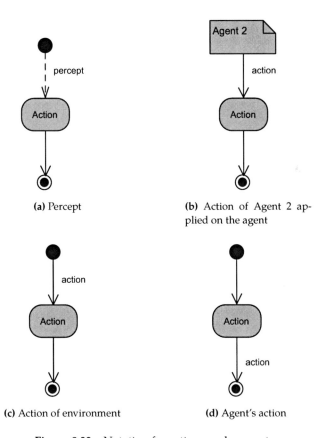

(a) Percept

(b) Action of Agent 2 applied on the agent

(c) Action of environment

(d) Agent's action

Figure 8.32 – Notation for actions and percepts

Actions and percepts are the kinds of interactions that can be simply depicted in an activity diagram as a standard starting (or ending) event with the caption representing the name of the message. In the case of a percept, the line is dashed (see Figure 8.32a). Actions of other agents applied to the agent are represented by an arrow from another agent's rectangle (see Figure 8.32b). Actions of the environment imposed on an agent are represented by a starting event with respective caption. See Figure 8.32c. Action of an agent on other agents or environments is depicted with an arrow to a rectangle of another agent (Figure 8.32d) or ending event respectively. In order to distinguish, for example, an action call from a regular end of the process, the ending (or starting) events representing actions must be captioned.

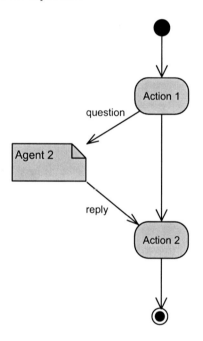

Figure 8.33 – Process of communication

Communication as one of the agent interactions is little bit more complicated. Communication itself is a process. We use communication diagrams for the description of the whole communication and an activity diagram for the representation of "what happens" on both sides (see Figure 8.33). The interaction consists of a set of outgoing and incoming messages that are modeled as arrows from and to a rectangle representing the second agent.

Example

As an example of an activity diagram in the agent conceptual model there is an elaboration of Traffic Observation behavior from Figure 8.34. The diagram is rather simple. It starts with a viewpoint percept which is processed concurrently in two branches. In the Update position action, the position (coordinates, direction and velocity) of the agent in the environment is simply updated. In the second branch, the noticed obstacles are processed. If the obstacle is already present in the map, its data are just updated to the current values. If it is not yet in the map, the obstacle is added.

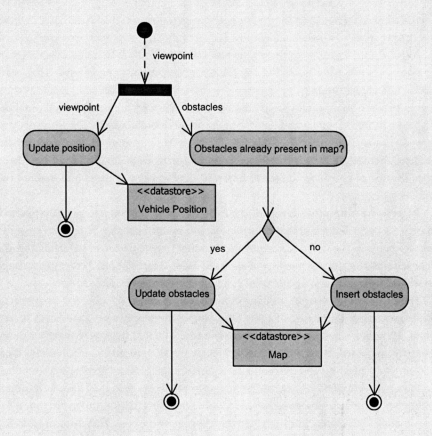

Figure 8.34 – An example of agent conceptual activity diagram

8.4   Drawbacks

The author of the methodology is aware of its drawbacks and limitations. First and fore-most, the purpose of the methodology was to make design and development of agent-based simulations easier, faster, cheaper and more feasible for a wider audience, including non-experts in IT. Although the first three objectives were met, the latter was satisfied just to a certain extent. The main reason is most likely low standardization of the industry. There is still no standard for agents, environments and many other issues in this field. The differences among the individual agent platforms are so wide that if the methodology should be universal and platform-independent, it has to be very general. The purpose of any methodology is generally to make things simpler, to set down the process of development and to provide best practices to avoid mistakes that somebody has already made. This then allows a wider set of much less experienced workforce to participate in the task, which makes the task cheaper. If this is true, it seems that standardization is what has made the object-oriented approach so successful. High standardization allows diminishing gaps between conceptual and platform-specific analysis or even between analysis and programming, and that is why, for example, agile methodologies were able to appear and flourish in the object-oriented world. The realm of agent technologies is far from such a situation, which makes any methodology very general and hence requires a high level of professional experience to develop agent-based systems, in turn diminishing the set of potential developers and users and making this technology expensive.

What we can do is an issue to consider further. The first option is to tailor the methodology for a particular agent platform. This would make it simpler, but due to large differences between the frameworks and a substantial fragmentation of the field, it would make it useless for the vast majority of potential users. Another option is to push through a standard for agents and agent-based simulations. This can be done in two ways.

The first is to implement a de jure standard by a generally accepted standardization organization. In the case of agent technologies there were several attempts at such action, all with limited success. The problem could be that they were mainly focused generally on the whole agent world, which made the attempt disputable. It seems there is no single agent world and the particular agent technologies and applications (robotics, mobile agents, simulations, etc.) differ in many more traits than they have in common. Authors of methodologies indeed often strive to see the big picture, but in fact they often serve mainly their own application field that they know the best. Therefore an approach focused strictly on the field of agent-based modeling could perhaps bring better results.

The second way is to implement a de facto standard; that is, a standard that has established itself due to its qualities, the market power of its authors or other reasons. Nowadays, the spectrum of agent platforms is very fragmented and perhaps no vendor considers agent-based simulations promising enough to push the technology. Given these reasons it does not seem there will emerge a standard in this way. In future the situation could change.

Another problem of Agentology is its tight connection with UML. This is both an advantage and disadvantage. The advantage is (as was mentioned above) that the costs of training and implementation of this methodology are considerably lower than if everything was invented from scratch – especially in the case that members of a development team are already familiar with UML and other modeling techniques. The disadvantage is that for people who have no prior experience with software modeling, training of this methodology is even more demanding, because they have to master not one, but two languages and methodologies at once.

Despite the drawbacks mentioned above, Agentology could still be a beneficial methodology for the field of agent-based modeling.

8.5 Chapter summary

One of the problems that prevents agent-based modeling as a method from a wider expansion is a lack of a relevant methodology for its development. Agentology should fill this gap. There are six roles defined: expert, analyst, modeler, platform specialist, programmer and tester. The design and development process consists of four phases and nine steps. Some of them are mandatory and others can be skipped or reduced. In the first step, the problem is formulated as a task for a solution. Next, the task should be evaluated for the most appropriate method of its solution. Then the conceptual modeling step is done. Its result is a conceptual – that is, a platform-independent – model of the system. It should be checked for its consistency in the next step and then the platform for the development should be selected. If there does not yet exist a guide for transformation of the conceptual model into the platform-specific model, it should be prepared next. A design of the platform-specific model is done then. In the last phase, the mere agent-based simulation is developed and finally evaluated for its conformance with reality.

For the purposes of agent conceptual modeling several diagrams were developed. Perhaps the most important is the agent diagram, which depicts agents in the system and their relationships. The environment diagram contains the description of interaction of the environment with agents. On a lower level of granularity, particle diagrams describe the individual aspects of agents, and these include agent class diagrams, communication diagrams and activity diagrams.

Agentology has also certain drawbacks. Even with the methodology, development of the agent-based simulation is still a challenging task that needs skilled professionals. Another problem is its use of some UML diagrams, which represents a requirement for further experience. In spite of these problems, Agentology could be still a beneficial methodology for the developers of agent-based simulations.

Appendix A

Jackson Structured Programming

A Jackson Structured Programming (JSP) diagram was used in this book. Although it has no role in Agentology methodology itself (see chapter 8) and is by no means critical for the understanding of this text, it is mentioned in an example that can be valuable for the reader. Because structured methodologies and particularly JSP belong to the instruments that are not very frequent anymore, the purpose of this appendix is to provide a brief introduction. The text below is definitely no comprehensive guide to JSP (one can be found, for example, in Jackson's Principles of Program Design[1]). This is rather a brief explanation of the constructs that are used in the text of this book. The program in JSP is structured using four elements:

- Fundamental operations

- Sequences

- Selections

- Iterations

Using these elements, any program structure could be described. The basic orientation in the charts is as follows: the program flow is depicted from left to right. Program structure is depicted top-down, which means that there is the most general and complex operation on the top, and on the lower, the more specific operations.

Basic elements of JSP diagrams are operations depicted as boxes. If we need to describe the internal structure of the operation, we use another (lower) row of operations (boxes) that are connected with lines. The leftmost operation is executed first; next the one on the right side of it is performed, and so on. See Figure A.1.

Selection is depicted as a box with a small circle in the top right corner. The individual cases of selection are on the same row connected with lines. There can be a note with the condition near the box. See Figure A.2.

Iteration is depicted as a box with a small asterisk in the top right corner. There can be a note with the number of iterations or the condition of the loop near the box. See Figure A.3.

---

[1]Jackson 1975.

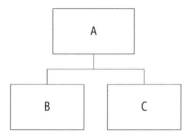

Figure A.1 – The operation A consists of operations B and C that will be executed sequentially (B first, then C).

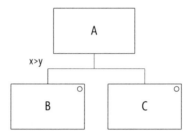

Figure A.2 – The operation A can be performed two ways. If the condition x>y matches, B will be executed. Otherwise C will be executed.

Some operations can be highlighted by two vertical lines. They indicate that the operation is a procedure, which means it can be called from other places in the code. See Figure A.4.

There is an example of a JSP diagram in Figure A.5. The procedure A consists of three steps (operations). First operation B is executed, then C. If the variable x equals 10, then E is performed, which means G is run five times. Otherwise (if x does not equal 10) F is executed. Finally, D is done.

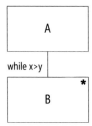

Figure A.3 – The operation A can be performed as a repetitive execution of B as long as x>y.

Figure A.4 – The operation A is a procedure; that is, a part of code that could be called from other places in the code.

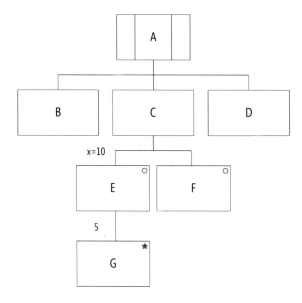

Figure A.5 – An example of Jackson Structured Programming diagram.

Appendix B
Agent-based modeling software

The theory of agency encompasses a wide range of problems, including design of agents, their interaction, learning and communication. Some of them were more or less deeply discussed in the previous chapters. If we want to apply any theory and use it for a particular purpose, we need a tool that implements it for a practical use. In the case of agent-based simulations, various frameworks, toolkits and agent development environments play this role. In this chapter, we will categorize them, introduce some examples and discover some of their limitations. Of course, it is possible to develop and operate a working multi-agent system without any tool on an ad hoc basis, and many systems are actually developed this way. Nonetheless, this chapter will omit this alternative.

The purpose of this chapter is not to provide "market research" of agent frameworks, but to unveil features and capabilities and current trends in this kind of software. The results will be used for a further analysis in the subsequent chapters of this book.

In recent years, several dozens of agent-based simulation tools were developed. For better lucidity, we will classify them into certain groups. There are many possible parameters that we can use for such a classification. The main aim is to provide a big picture of the present state of these tools.

The list of the frameworks introduced in the following text is definitely not complete (at least because of their continually-growing number), but the author's intent is that it should be representative as much as possible. It is also necessary to stress that although all of the following frameworks can be used for agent-based simulation, not all are intended primarily for that purpose.

The tools will be classified according to the following categories:

- *Environment* – there are generally two main kinds of tools: toolkits with a user environment or even an integrated development environment (IDE), and libraries that lack the environment.[1] Toolkits are much easier for training and using, because users often do not need a deep knowledge of programming and agent architectures, so they can focus on the agent-based model itself. On the other hand, the users are constrained with the abilities of the tool much more than in the case of libraries, and the performance is often worse because the environment itself consumes some part of the system resources. Libraries typically provide agent-related

---

[1] "Toolkits" and "libraries" are just working names, not generally established terms.

library functions or classes for a certain programming language. Developers are much freer in their work, but using the library is considerably more difficult than in the case of toolkits, because programming skills are necessary.

- *Architecture* – in chapter 3 there were presented the main types of agent architecture. Some tools are specialized in a certain method, while others can support more approaches.

- *Simulation language* – unlike some other kinds of simulation software, none of the present tools is fully visual. Users always need to use certain textual programming language to develop agents or at least some of their aspects. In the case of libraries, the use of programming language is indeed implied. Various languages are used; some of them are described separately, for example AgentSpeak(L), and some were developed particularly for the respective tool (e.g., Visual AgentTalk).

- *Platform* – besides simulation language, the platform on which the tool was developed is often important as well. Some tools expect the use of two languages: a simulation language and a language of the platform in order to compile the model. For instance, Jason needs the agents written in Agent-Speak(L), and their working environment and other code written in Java, which runs under Jason itself. The platform also tells us a lot about the possible overall performance and other capabilities of the system (Java-based platforms, for instance, provide typically significantly weaker performance than for example the platforms based on C++, due to properties of the language).

- *Specification* – several common standards of multi-agent frameworks have been developed. They were discussed in chapter 3. Some of the tools incorporate a specific standard and the others are developed on an ad hoc basis.

- *Scale* – although one would guess that multi-agent systems and agent-based simulations must be huge software systems, the contrary is the case. Most of the simulation tools are desktop applications and hence their capacity is limited by the performance of the system they run on (we will class them among *small* systems). Other tools implement networking capabilities and can form larger structures by connecting agents hosted on more physical computers. Let's call them *scalable* systems. The last category is *mega-scale* systems that support huge agent-based models that are occupied by millions of agents. Due to tremendous requirements on their computational power and advanced networking composition, hardly any of the commonly available frameworks are able to back this kind of system. All agent-based models of this size that are known to the author of this book were developed so far on an ad hoc basis. Unfortunately, as will be mentioned in chapter 7.5 on page 99, for some applications of agent based simulations, systems of this size are necessary.

It is not easy to sort the tools according to any taxonomy, because there is seldom a clear distinction between the categories. When in doubt, the tool was assigned to the closest group.

B.1   Examining agent frameworks

To obtain the list of software for categorization, a meta-analysis of several papers that provide the evaluation or comparison of various agent tools was conducted. Even if there were more than 70 tools in the list initially, it was definitely far from being complete and it was surely possible to find dozens of other tools with further effort, from other sources. However, the list can never be complete, because new tools emerge and some others are being discontinued from time to time.

The sources for the following meta-analysis were the articles of Allan,[2] Perdikeas et al.,[3] Nguyen et al.,[4] and Nikolai et al.[5] These articles cover most of the relevant agent frameworks for the last 10 years. In order to keep the analysis up to date, the projects mentioned in the articles that were discontinued have been removed from the list, and the final number of surveyed frameworks was 46. Because about one third of the projects had ceased, but presumably other tens of frameworks were started, it seems that the field of agent-based simulation software is still in the development and experimental phase and far from being mature.

Even if we set aside the tools that were not included into this research because they were not cited in the aforementioned articles, the number of 46 "living" projects may not be correct, because it is not often clear whether the software is still supported or if it was already abandoned, as some of the tools were not updated for several years. Therefore, the criterion of existing Web presentation was used. If the project has its Web site with information about the framework, documentation, and so on, it is considered "living"; otherwise it is deemed discontinued. This approach is not entirely correct as a method, but it can be considered a good proxy for the purposes of this survey. The list of living frameworks (with measures of their influence – see below) appears in Figure B.1.

It would not be correct to treat all the frameworks in the list equally. As in any other category of software, some are more important and well established than others. The influence of tools varies; some are widespread and have thousands of users, some are just experimental projects with several applications that are used (almost) solely just by their own authors. In business applications, market share is often a common measure of influence. In the field of agent frameworks, such data are lacking, because of the primarily academic and experimental role of these tools. It is not easy to evaluate their

---

[2]Allan 2009.
[3]Perdikeas, Chatzipapadopoulos, and Venieris 1999.
[4]Nguyen et al. 2002.
[5]Nikolai and Madey 2009.

influence, though it is a very important indicator. For our purposes, three methods were employed:

- *Citations* – the more articles, conference papers and other material about the subject, probably the more important is the subject matter. For purposes of this book, research on the Scopus citation database[6] was conducted. Scopus contains about 18,000 titles of scholarly literature and hence it is a good body of data for such a survey. The number of relevant articles found is the score.

- *Google* – these days, Google is among the most important search engines, with billions of indexed documents with a wide variety of content. As everything from blogs and personal pages to corporate Web sites, libraries, and so on are indexed, the overall quality of information is probably lower than in the case of a scholarly citation database. On the other hand, for those kinds of agent frameworks that are commercially developed and marketed, Google can be a more relevant resource than Scopus, because they can be less covered or even ignored by scientific data sources. The number of documents found is the score for this category.

- *Author's "expert opinion"* – the aforementioned indicators work with a certain algorithm that could be biased for many reasons (see below). Expert opinion can be valuable, as the expert knows how often he or she meets with the individual frameworks and how important are they in the relevant community. On the other hand, this method is inevitably subjective and the results are influenced by the expert's attitudes and surroundings.

Survey methodology was as follows: in the case of Scopus, the name of framework was used as a keyword. The word "agent" was used as a supplemental keyword. If there were more than 90% of irrelevant results, "multi-agent system" was used instead of "agent." Merely using the longer phrase would imply a less sensitive search, and using the shorter phrase would return many irrelevant outcomes. In the case of Google, the search query consisted of the name of the framework with the supplemental words "agent framework." Because there are many acronyms and abbreviations with a special meaning used as the names of frameworks (like LSD, Zeus, Brahms, Jason, JAM, etc.), which leads to false results, full names of frameworks (LSD – Laboratory for Simulation Development) or other distinctive keywords (Zeus Agent Building Toolkit) were used instead of abbreviations. The drawback of this approach is that the specific phrase has a substantial impact on the outcome of the search. It brings a subjective element to this method. Expert opinion was the first method that was used. The author of this book wrote down all the frameworks he did remember without any notes. Then he scored all of the frameworks on the list between 1 and 10 (where 10 is the maximum) according to

---

[6]See http://www.scopus.com (visited on 9.6.2010)

their importance from the author's point of view. All other frameworks that were not on the author's list but were on the list of evaluated frameworks got zero. The fit among the methods was tested with a correlation coefficient. In an ideal case all the methods should bring the same results; that is, their correlation coefficient should be 1. In this case the correlation between the citations and Google was 0.95, between Google and "expert" it was 0.66 and between "expert" and citations it was 0.75. It is possible to say that there is a strong positive relationship and so the results are credible.

The methodology of the survey (see Table B.1 and Figure B.1) is as follows. For three aforementioned measures we get three factors: $x_{s}c$ indicating the number of citations on Scopus, x_g indicating the number of hits on Google and $x_{e}o$ indicating the expert opinion in the range between 0 and 10. On this basis we calculate the measure of influence as an average of the particular factors. Each factor participates as a percentage of the value and the maximum of the factor. All factors have the same weight. The formula B.1 was used.

$$\bar{x} = \frac{1}{3}\left(\frac{x_{sc}}{\max x_{sc}} + \frac{x_g}{\max x_g} + \frac{x_{eo}}{\max x_{eo}} \right)$$ (B.1)

Influence is a dimensionless number. By itself, it does not say much, but the proportions between the influences of various frameworks are interesting.

Table B.1 – Measures of influence of surveyed agent frameworks.

Framework	x_{sc}	x_g	x_{eo}	$\bar{x}$	Framework	x_{sc}	x_g	x_{eo}	$\bar{x}$
ABLE[7]	3	173	0	0.005	Jason[8]	2	5560	0	0.055
AgentBuilder[9]	1	1380	0	0.014	LSD[10]	0	212	0	0.002
AgentSheets[11]	2	3110	0	0.032	MadKit[12]	0	1810	0	0.017
Aglets[13]	36	5610	0	0.099	MAML[14]	0	645	0	0.006
A-Globe[15]	3	2920	0	0.031	MASON[16]	3	143	3	0.105
Ajanta[17]	2	1820	0	0.020	MASS[18]	0	10	0	0.000
Anylogic[19]	0	741	3	0.107	MIMOSE[20]	0	445	0	0.004
Ascape[21]	0	965	2	0.076	Moduleco[22]	0	223	0	0.002
Brahms[23]	5	242	0	0.009	NetLogo[24]	19	1150	5	0.202
Breve[25]	0	1810	0	0.017	Omonia[26]	0	158	0	0.001
Cormas[27]	1	1410	0	0.015	Ps-i[28]	0	3220	0	0.030
Cougaar[29]	12	2390	3	0.138	Repast[30]	13	3510	8	0.317
deX[31]	0	183	0	0.002	SeSAm[32]	1	1980	0	0.020
D-OMAR[33]	0	235	0	0.002	SimAgent[34]	0	322	0	0.003
EcoLab[35]	0	1530	0	0.014	Soar[36]	0	1120	0	0.011
FAMOJA[37]	0	74	0	0.001	Spark[38]	3	920	0	0.013
FLAME[39]	0	70	0	0.001	StarLogo[40]	0	6360	1	0.094
JACK[41]	16	2240	2	0.108	Swarm[42]	260	35200	10	1.000
JADE[43]	110	9790	10	0.567	Tryllian[44]	0	565	0	0.005
JADEX[45]	8	3450	0	0.043	VisualBots[46]	0	336	0	0.003
JAM[47]	6	1150	0	0.019	VSEit[48]	0	148	0	0.001
JAS[49]	0	4560	0	0.043	Xholon[50]	0	139	0	0.001
JASA[51]	0	330	0	0.003	Zeus[52]	7	515	0	0.014

The results of the survey say that there are few well-established frameworks (the impact of the three most influential is higher than the impact of all other tools together), and many other tools with minor success. In fact, there are probably many more marginal tools, but they were not included in the research for the reasons mentioned above. In Ta-

---

[7]http://www.alphaworks.ibm.com/tech/able
[8]http://jason.sourceforge.net
[9]http://www.agentbuilder.com
[10]http://www.labsimdev.org
[11]http://www.agentsheets.com
[12]http://www.madkit.org
[13]http://www.trl.ibm.com/aglets
[14]http://www.maml.hu
[15]http://agents.felk.cvut.cz
[16]http://www.cs.gmu.edu/~eclab/projects/mason
[17]http://ajanta.cs.umn.edu
[18]http://mass.aitia.ai
[19]http://www.xjtek.com
[20]http://www.uni-koblenz.de/~moeh/projekte/mimose.html
[21]http://ascape.sourceforge.net
[22]http://www.cs.manchester.ac.uk/ai/public/moduleco
[23]http://www.agentsolutions.com
[24]http://ccl.northwestern.edu/netlogo
[25]http://www.spiderland.org
[26]http://www.xlog.ch/omonia
[27]http://cormas.cirad.fr
[28]http://ps-i.sourceforge.net
[29]http://cougaar.org
[30]http://repast.sourceforge.net
[31]http://dextk.org
[32]http://www.simsesam.de
[33]http://omar.bbn.com
[34]http://www.cs.bham.ac.uk/research/projects/poplog/packages/simagent.html
[35]http://ecolab.sourceforge.net
[36]http://sitemaker.umich.edu/soar/home
[37]http://www.usf.uni-osnabrueck.de/projects/famoja
[38]http://www.ai.sri.com/~spark
[39]https://trac.flame.ac.uk
[40]http://education.mit.edu/starlogo
[41]http://www.aosgrp.com.au/products/jack
[42]http://www.swarm.org
[43]http://jade.tilab.com
[44]http://www.tryllian.org
[45]http://jadex.sourceforge.net
[46]http://www.visualbots.com
[47]http://www.marcush.net/IRS/irs_downloads.html
[48]http://www.vseit.de
[49]http://jaslibrary.sourceforge.net
[50]http://www.primordion.com/Xholon
[51]http://jasa.sourceforge.net
[52]http://labs.bt.com/projects/agents/zeus

ble B.2 there is a list of agent frameworks sorted according to their calculated influence. The same information is in Figure B.1.

Table B.2 – List of frameworks sorted according to their calculated influence.

Framework	Influence	Framework	Influence
Swarm	100.0%	EcoLab	1.4%
JADE	56.7%	AgentBuilder	1.4%
Repast	31.7%	Zeus	1.4%
NetLogo	20.2%	Spark	1.3%
Cougaar	13.8%	Soar	1.1%
JACK	10.8%	Brahms	0.9%
Anylogic	10.7%	MAML	0.6%
MASON	10.5%	ABLE	0.5%
Aglets	9.9%	Tryllian	0.5%
StarLogo	9.4%	MIMOSE	0.4%
Ascape	7.6%	VisualBots	0.3%
Jason	5.5%	JASA	0.3%
JAS	4.3%	SimAgent	0.3%
JADEX	4.3%	D-OMAR	0.2%
AgentSheets	3.2%	Moduleco	0.2%
A-Globe	3.1%	LSD	0.2%
Ps-i	3.0%	deX	0.2%
SeSAm	2.0%	Omonia	0.1%
Ajanta	2.0%	VSEit	0.1%
JAM	1.9%	Xholon	0.1%
Breve	1.7%	FAMOJA	0.1%
MadKit	1.7%	FLAME	0.1%
Cormas	1.5%	MASS	0.0%

    As we can see, the influence is very unequal. The awareness of the first three frameworks is about the same as of the remaining 43. The compound influence of the first 10 frameworks is more than 8 times higher than of all the rest (they are **bolded** in the subsequent tables). This means that there emerged a couple of leaders in the field that are much more important than the others. On the other hand, the field is still under development, as a high number of tools is available.

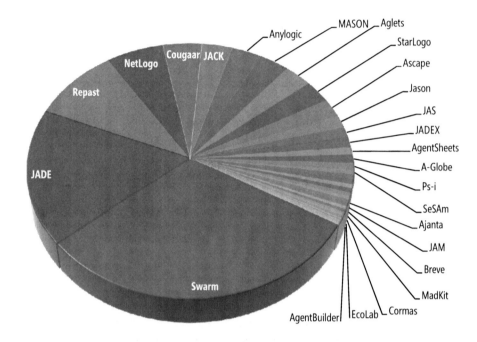

Figure B.1 – Influence of agent frameworks

B.2   User environment

As mentioned above, it is not always clear whether the tool has the (graphical) user environment or not. Some of the library distributions contain, for example, development, monitoring or other utilities with the user environment; some toolkit environments, on the other hand, are not much more than simple text editors, Eclipse plug-ins, and so on. If the user environment is an important feature of the software, it is considered a toolkit in the following categorization; otherwise it is included among libraries.

From a tool-user's point of view, it is much more difficult to develop simulations with libraries than by using toolkits, as he or she needs to write a code in programming language. On the other hand, libraries can typically offer a better and wider set of features, so they are more universal.

Although it is more challenging to develop toolkits than libraries, there are more toolkits available, as we can see from the Table B.3. Because we discuss tools that are intended to be used primarily by social sciences researchers (i.e., not IT specialists), user-friendliness is a valuable and demanded feature, and hence the number of toolkits is greater than the number of libraries among multi-agent frameworks.

There are considerably more influential tools among frameworks (7) than among libraries (3).

Table B.3 – Classification according to the presence of user environment.

Toolkits (with environment)		Libraries (without environment)	
ABLE	AgentBuilder	Aglets	A-Globe
AgentSheets	Anylogic	Ajanta	Brahms
Ascape	Breve	Cougaar	deX
Cormas	D-OMAR	EcoLab	FLAME
JACK	JAS	FAMOJA	JADE
Jason	LSD	JADEX	JAM
MAML	MASON	JASA	MadKit
MASS	MIMOSE	Omonia	SimAgent
Moduleco	NetLogo	Soar	Spark
Ps-i	Repast	Tryllian	Zeus
SeSAm	StarLogo family		
Swarm	VSEit		
VisualBots	Xholon		

B.3 Architecture

After reading the previous chapters, one could think that the architecture of a multi-agent system is a distinctive characteristic. Nonetheless, the contrary is the case. Regarding agent architecture, there are two main kinds of agent frameworks: first, those that are based on a specific architecture; and second, general tools that embody no special agent concept and can support agents based on almost any principle. The first group of tools consists of formal agent frameworks that provide elegant, semantically grounded models of agent behavior.[53] Unfortunately, they are often not used for real problems except their self-presentation. The only specific agent architecture that represents a notable influence is Belief-Desire-Intention.[54] The vast majority of real applications of agent-based simulations work with no specific architecture and users are free to build their models on any principles they want.

As mentioned above, except BDI there is no particular architecture used in agent-based frameworks. JACK is probably the only framework based on BDI with a significant influence. A majority of frameworks (including the most cited) do not support and provide any specific architecture.

The development of a tool without any particular incorporated architecture is typically simpler than using a specific architecture like BDI. Analysts have more freedom to build their models on a generic system; however they have to take more effort.

---

[53]Morley and Myers 2004.
[54]See 3.4.3

Table B.4 – Classification according to the system architecture.

No specific architecture		BDI	
ABLE	AgentBuilder	Brahms	**JACK**
AgentSheets	A-Globe	JADEX	JAM
Ajanta	**Anylogic**	Jason	Spark
Ascape	Breve		
Cormas	**Cougaar**		
deX	D-OMAR		
EcoLab	FLAME		
FAMOJA	**JADE**		
JAS	JASA		
LSD	MadKit		
MAML	**MASON**		
MASS	MIMOSE		
Moduleco	**NetLogo**		
Ps-i	Omonia		
Repast	SeSAm		
SimAgent	Soar		
StarLogo family	**Swarm**		
Tryllian	VSEit		
VisualBots	Xholon		
Zeus			

B.4   Simulation language

Even agent language is not so clear a parameter of the agent framework as one could guess. Agent tools typically use various languages for various purposes. They frequently use a platform language merely for the framework (environment), and a language for development of agents (this often has the syntax of logic language), but there other languages can also be used for communication (KIF, KQML), for representing ontologies and for other purposes. In the following tables, the tools are grouped according to the language in which the agents are coded.

As we can see, most of tools use their own language designated especially for such a purpose. The advantage of this concept is that the tool with a special language can provide unique capabilities. On the other hand, learning a new language for a particular platform is costly.

---

[55] ARL language
[56] RADL language
[57] Visual AgentTalk language
[58] steve language
[59] SCORE language
[60] MAML language
[61] FABLES language

Table B.5 – Classification according to the simulation language.

own		Java	
ABLE[55]	AgentBuilder[56]	Aglets	A-Globe
AgentSheets[57]	AnyLogic	Ajanta	Ascape
Brahms	Breve[58]	Cougaar	FAMOJA
Cormas	deX	JACK	JADE
D-OMAR[59]	JAM	JADEX	JAS
Jason	MAML[60]	JASA	MadKit
MASS[61]	MIMOSE	MASON	Moduleco
Ps-i	Omonia	Repast	Swarm
SeSAm	Soar	Tryllian	Zeus
Spark	VSEit		
C/C++/Objective-C		Logo	
EcoLab	FLAME	NetLogo	StarLogo family
LSD	Swarm		
Pop-11/Poplog		Visual Basic	
SimAgent		VisualBots	
UML			
Xholon			

There is Java on the second position and the reason is probably that Java technologies are by far the most frequent platform of agent frameworks (see below) and so it is easy for their developers to employ it as the simulation language. Note that the vast majority of the most successful tools use Java. Among the other substantial languages of agent-based simulations are the C family of languages and Logo.

The number of simulation languages as well as the number of special languages of the individual tools indicate that this kind of software is not well standardized so far. The author considers it problematic that there are no significant simulation languages for agent-based simulations, because this hinders the wider spread of this technology. Using programming languages like Java or even C-like languages for simulation purposes is not very convenient either, because they are relatively hard to learn for non-programmers, lack some important features of agent-oriented programming and contain many attributes that are not needed for this purpose.

B.5 Platform

By platform we mean a language and software environment the agents operate on (such as Java/JRE). This characteristic is relatively easy to distinguish.

As can be clearly seen, Java technology is the number-one platform. There are far more frameworks based on Java than on all other technologies combined. In the second

---

[62]Swarm exists in versions for both Java and Objective-C.

Table B.6 – Classification according to the platform.

Java technologies		C/C++/Objective-C	
ABLE	AgentBuilder	deX	EcoLab
AgentSheets	Aglets	FLAME	LSD
A-Globe	Ajanta	MAML	Ps-i
AnyLogic	Ascape	Soar	Swarm[62]
Brahms	Cougaar		
D-OMAR	FAMOJA		
JACK	JADE		
JADEX	JAM		
JAS	Jason		
JASA	Madit		
MASON	MASS		
MIMOSE	Moduleco		
NetLogo	Omonia		
Repast	SeSAm		
Soar	Spark		
Starlogo family	Swarm		
Tryllian	VSEit		
Xholon	Zeus		
SmallTalk		Python	
Cormas		Breve	Soar
Lisp		Poplog/Pop-11	
D-OMAR		SimAgent	
Visual Basic			
VisualBots			

position are tools based on C/C++/Objective-C, and all other technologies are negligible.

The main advantage of Java is that it is ubiquitous, offers many development tools and libraries for free, is relatively easy to learn (and very commonly taught at universities) and allows rapid development. Unfortunately, Java's substantial problem is that it is slow, which disqualifies it from any high-performance application.

B.6　Specification

In the 90s several attempts to unify standards in the multi-agent community occurred and various standards of agent technologies (including FIPA,[63] OMG MASIF,[64] KAoS,[65] Open Agent Architecture,[66] etc. were issued. Later the concern for agent standardization

---

[63]See http://www.fipa.org (visited on 9.6.2010)
[64]*Mobile Agent System Interoperability Facilities Specification* 1997.
[65]Bradshaw et al. 1997.
[66]Cheyer and Martin 2001.

faded away slightly. In the following table the agent frameworks are grouped according to the standard they follow (if any). Lists in the following table are based on the manifested compliance with the particular standards. Their real compliance was not tested for the purposes of this survey. vast majority of contemporary agent frameworks

Table B.7 – Classification according to the standards employed.

No standard		FIPA	
ABLE	AgentBuilder	A-Globe (limited)	JACK
AgentSheets	Ajanta	JADE	JADEX
AnyLogic	Ascape	JAS	Tryllian
Brahms	Breve	Zeus	
Cormas	Cougaar		
deX	D-OMAR		
Ecolab	FAMOJA		
JAM	JASA		
Jason	LSD		
MAML	MASON		
MASS	MIMOSE		
Moduleco	NetLogo		
Ps-i	Omonia		
Repast	SeSAm		
SimAgent	Soar		
Spark	Starlogo family		
Swarm	VSEit		
VisualBots	Xholon		
OMG MASIF			
Aglets			

do not follow any standard. The most applied are FIPA standards, but agent tools that employ them are still rare (although there are some influential frameworks like JADE or JACK among them). The only existing framework obeying the OMG MASIF standard are IBM's Agelts, as others were discontinued (e.g., Grasshopper). The author did not find any existing framework implementing any of other standards. This could be interpreted as an unsuitability of the existing standards, because it seems to be a better option for most developers to offer a non-standard solutions.

B.7 Scale

Multi-agent frameworks are either standalone, distributed (scalable) or large (called mega-scale or exa-scale, meaning the same category). As in the case of other characteristics, distinction of system scale is not straightforward, because there are no sharp dividing lines among the particular categories. Many "standalone" systems possess certain networking capabilities, and the level of "distributedness" of distributed frameworks, on the other hand, can vary substantially. The distinction between distributed and large tools is even vaguer. A working definition of a "large," mega-scale framework is that it is able to operate smoothly at least 10^6 plus agents (but more preferably 10^7, 10^8 and higher orders). Standalone simulation tools are more common

Table B.8 – Classification according to the size of the system.

Standalone		Distributed	
AgentBuilder Lite	AgentSheets	ABLE	AgentBuilder Pro
AnyLogic	Breve	Aglets	A-Globe
Cormas	FAMOJA	Ajanta	Brahms
JACK	JAM	Cougaar	deX
JASA	Jason	D-OMAR	EcoLab
LSD	MAML	JADE	JADEX
MASON	MASS	JAS	SeSAm
MIMOSE	Moduleco	SimAgent	Soar
NetLogo	Ps-i	Tryllian	Zeus
Omonia	Repast		
Spark	Starlogo family		
Swarm	VSEit		
VisualBots	Xholon		
Large			
FLAME			

than distributed ones and many of the most successful systems are among them. It is no wonder, as they are simpler to develop and use and there is no need for distributedness in many particular applications (e.g., for education purposes). However, there are many tools using distributed architecture and therefore allowing the execution of larger simulations. The capacity of most of them is nonetheless limited and their performance drops significantly with the number of running agents or computers integrated into the system (problems regarding building big multi-agent systems are mentioned in section 7.5).

There was just one member in the category of large frameworks and its inclusion in this category is also questionable. Truly large agent-based simulations are still an issue due to numerous technical difficulties, and existing systems are typically built on an ad hoc basis. Such systems include, for example, exa-scale simulations developed at Argonne National Laboratory[67] or the EpiSimS system developed at Los Alamos National Laboratory,[68] among others.

---

[67]North et al. 2008.
[68]Stroud et al. 2007.

B.8   Chapter summary

There is a large gap between the theory of agency and practical agent tools. On one hand there is a well-developed and sound theory; on the other hand, in reality, the tools are far behind it, or theory and practice even go different ways. Theory offers several concepts of agency, but no one of them seems to be dominant. Except certain support of BDI, all real agent tools are general and leave the decision about agent architecture completely up to the developer of the simulation. There are more small, standalone tools than those that support distributed architecture. It means that the capacity of the simulations created in such systems is limited and it is not possible to develop big, high-performance models.

The same problem stems from the dominant position of Java technology among agent technologies, which dramatically curtails the feasible performance of the system. The advantage of Java is definitely its simplicity and the convenience for educative purposes; however its suitability for this type of application is questionable. It is not surprising that there are many academic institutions among the developers of the tools for agent-based simulation.[69]

We can conclude that although there are a high number of possible tools for agent-based simulation, most of them are suitable for education, research and experimental purposes, and there is a lack of systems that can be used for big, real-world simulations. This is probably the reason why the successful agent-based models, instead of some of the tools, are often conducted on ad hoc systems.

---

[69] ČVUT (A-Globe), University of Minnesota (Ajanta), Arizona State University (DEVS), Universität Osnabrück (FAMOJA), George Mason University (MASON), Koblenz-Landau Universität (Mimose), Northwestern University (NetLogo), University of Birmingham (SimAgent), University of Michigan (Soar), Massachusetts Institute of Technology (StarLogo), etc. Among the non-academic institutions, there are IBM (ABLE, Aglets), Telecom Italia (JADE), British Telecom (Zeus), NASA (Brahms), DARPA (Cougaar), etc.

Bibliography

Allan, Rob J. (June 2009). *Survey of Agent Based Modelling and Simulation Tools.* Tech. rep. STFC Daresbury Laboratory. URL: http://epubs.cclrc.ac.uk/work-details?w=50398. (Cit. on p. 175).

Ambastha, Madhur et al. (2005). "Evolving a Multiagent System for Landmark-Based Robot Navigation". In: *International Journal of Intelligent Systems* 20, pp. 523–539. (Cit. on p. 14).

Biswas, Pratik K. (2008). "Towards an agent-oriented approach to conceptualization". In: *Appl. Soft Comput.* 8.1, pp. 127–139. ISSN: 1568-4946. DOI: http://dx.doi.org/10.1016/j.asoc.2006.11.009. (Cit. on p. 72).

Boero, Riccardo and Flaminio Squazzoni (2005). "Does Empirical Embeddedness Matter? Methodological Issues on Agent-Based Models for Analytical Social Science". In: *Journal of Artificial Societies and Social Simulation* 8, p. 4. URL: http://econpapers.repec.org/RePEc:jas:jasssj:2005-66-1. (Cit. on p. 98).

Bordini, Rafael H. and Jomi F. Hübner (Feb. 2007). *JASON - A Java-based interpreter for an extended version of AgentSpeak.* URL: http://jason.sourceforge.net/Jason.pdf. (Cit. on pp. 54–56).

Bradshaw, Jeffrey M. et al. (1997). "KAoS: toward an industrial-strength open agent architecture". In: pp. 375–418. (Cit. on p. 184).

Bratman, Michael E. (Mar. 1999). *Intention, Plans, and Practical Reason.* Cambridge University Press. ISBN: 1575861925. URL: http://www.amazon.com/exec/obidos/redirect?tag=citeulike07-20&path=ASIN/1575861925. (Cit. on p. 52).

Brenner, Thomas and Claudia Werker (2009). *Policy Advice Derived From Simulation Models.* MPRA Paper. University Library of Munich, Germany. URL: http://econpapers.repec.org/RePEc:pra:mprapa:13134. (Cit. on p. 18).

Bresciani, Paolo et al. (2004). "Tropos: An Agent-Oriented Software Development Methodology". In: *Autonomous Agents and Multi-Agent Systems* 8.3, pp. 203–236. ISSN: 1387-2532. DOI: http://dx.doi.org/10.1023/B:AGNT.0000018806.20944.ef. (Cit. on pp. 92, 93).

Brin, Sergey and Lawrence Page (1998). "The anatomy of a large-scale hypertextual Web search engine". In: *Comput. Netw. ISDN Syst.* 30.1-7, pp. 107–117. ISSN: 0169-7552. DOI: http://dx.doi.org/10.1016/S0169-7552(98)00110-X. (Cit. on p. 16).

Brooks, Rodney A. (1990). "Elephants Don't Play Chess". In: *Robotics and Autonomous Systems* 6, pp. 3–51. (Cit. on p. 31).

— (Aug. 1991a). "Intelligence Without Reason". In: *Proceedings of the 12th International Joint Conference on Artificial Intelligence*. Ed. by Ray Myopoulos, John; Reiter. Sydney, Australia: Morgan Kaufmann, pp. 569–595. ISBN: 1-55860-160-0. URL: http://www.ai.mit.edu/people/brooks/papers/AIM-1293.ps.z. (Cit. on p. 29).

— (1991b). "Intelligence without representation". In: *Artificial Intelligence* 47.1-3, pp. 139–159. ISSN: 0004-3702. DOI: http://dx.doi.org/10.1016/0004-3702(91)90053-M. (Cit. on p. 29).

Cahlík, Tomáš (2006). *Multiagentní přístupy v ekonomii*. UK Praha. ISBN: 80-246-1223-2. (Cit. on p. 6).

Campos, André M. C. et al. (2004). "MASim: A Methodology for the Development of Agent-based Simulations:" in: *Proceedings 16th European Simulation Symposium*. Ed. by György Lipovszki and István Molnár. (Cit. on pp. 89, 90).

Carley, Kathleen M. et al. (2006). "BioWar: Scalable Agent-Based Model of Bioattacks." In: *IEEE Transactions on Systems, Man, and Cybernetics, Part A* 36.2, pp. 252–265. URL: http://dblp.uni-trier.de/db/journals/tsmc/tsmca36.html#CarleyFCYACKN06. (Cit. on p. 18).

Caro, Gianni Di and Marco Dorigo (1998). "An adaptive multi-agent routing algorithm inspired by ants behavior". In: *In Proceedings of PART98 - 5th Annual Australasian Conference on Parallel and Real-Time Systems*. Springer-Verlag, pp. 261–272. (Cit. on p. 16).

Casal, Arancha (2000). "Multiagent Control of Self-Reconfigurable Robots". In: *ICMAS '00: Proceedings of the Fourth International Conference on MultiAgent Systems (ICMAS-2000)*. Washington, DC, USA: IEEE Computer Society, p. 143. ISBN: 0-7695-0625-9. (Cit. on p. 14).

Chaibdraa, Brahim and Jörg P. Müller (2006). *Multiagent based supply chain management*. Springer. ISBN: 3-540-33875-6=978-3-540-33875-8. URL: http://gso.gbv.de/DB=2.1/CMD?ACT=SRCHA&SRT=YOP&IKT=1016&TRM=ppn+510122361&sourceid=fbw_bibsonomy. (Cit. on p. 17).

Chen, Kan et al. (2005). "The Emergence of Racial Segregation in an Agent-Based Model of Residential Location: The Role of Competing Preferences". In: *Comput. Math. Organ. Theory* 11.4, pp. 333–338. ISSN: 1381-298X. DOI: http://dx.doi.org/10.1007/s10588-005-5588-4. (Cit. on p. 19).

Cheyer, Adam and David Martin (Mar. 2001). "The Open Agent Architecture". In: *Journal of Autonomous Agents and Multi-Agent Systems* 4.1. OAA, pp. 143–148. (Cit. on p. 184).

Cioffi-Revilla, Claudio (2002). "Invariance and Universality in Social Agent-Based Simulations". In: *Proceedings of the National Academy of Sciences of the United States of America*. Ed. by Arthur M. Sackler. Vol. 99. 10. National Academy of Sciences, pp. 7314–7316. (Cit. on p. 97).

Cioppa, Thomas M., Thomas W. Lucas, and Susan M. Sanchez (2004). "Military applications of agent-based simulations". In: *WSC '04: Proceedings of the 36th conference on Winter simulation*. Washington, D.C.: Winter Simulation Conference, pp. 171–180. ISBN: 0-7803-8786-4. (Cit. on p. 18).

Collinot, A., A. Drogoul, and P. Benhamou (Dec. 1996). "Agent Oriented Design of a Soccer Robot Team". In: *Proceedings of the Second International. Conference on Multi-Agent Systems*. Kyoto, Japan. (Cit. on p. 86).

Dahl, O. J., E. W. Dijkstra, and C. A. R. Hoare, eds. (1972). *Structured programming*. London, UK, UK: Academic Press Ltd. ISBN: 0-12-200550-3. (Cit. on p. 159).

DeLoach, Scott A., Mark F. Wood, and Clint H. Sparkman (2001). "Multiagent Systems Engineering". In: *International Journal of Software Engineering and Knowledge Engineering* 11.3, pp. 231–258. (Cit. on p. 89).

Dillon, Darshan S., Tharam S. Dillon, and Elizabeth Chang (2008). "Using UML 2.1 to Model Multi-agent Systems". In: *SEUS '08: Proceedings of the 6th IFIP WG 10.2 international workshop on Software Technologies for Embedded and Ubiquitous Systems*. Berlin, Heidelberg: Springer-Verlag, pp. 1–8. ISBN: 978-3-540-87784-4. DOI: http://dx.doi.org/10.1007/978-3-540-87785-1_1. (Cit. on p. 85).

Dlouhý, Martin, Jan Fábry, and Martina Kuncová (2005). *Simulace pro ekonomy*. Prague: Vysoká škola ekonomická. ISBN: 80-245-0973-3. (Cit. on pp. 6–8).

Dogac, Asuman et al. (1998). "Research and Advanced Technology for Digital Libraries". In: vol. 1513/1998. Lecture Notes in Computer Science. Springer. Chap. METU-EMar: An Agent-Based Electronic Marketplace on the Web, pp. 777–790. DOI: 10.1007/3-540-49653-X_80. (Cit. on p. 17).

Dresner, Kurt and Peter Stone (2006). "Learning and Adaption in Multi-Agent Systems". In: vol. 3898/2006. Lecture Notes in Computer Science. Berlin / Heidelberg: Springer. Chap. Multiagent Traffic Management: Opportunities for Multiagent Learning, pp. 129–138. DOI: 10.1007/11691839_7. (Cit. on p. 17).

Eigenmann, Rudolf and David J. Lilja (1999). "Von Neumann Computers". In: *Wiley Encyclopedia of Electrical and Electronics Engineering* 23, pp. 387–400. URL: http://www.ece.purdue.edu/~eigenman/reports/vN.pdf. (Cit. on p. 13).

Elammari, M. and W. Lalonde (June 1999). "An Agent-Oriented Methodology: High-Level and Intermediate Models". In: *Proceedings of AOIS 1999*. Heidelberg, Germany. (Cit. on p. 88).

Finin, Tim, Don McKay, and Rich Fritzson (1992). *An overview of KQML: A Knowledge Query and Manipulation Language*. Tech. rep. The KQML Advisory Group. (Cit. on p. 69).

FIPA ACL Message Structure Specification (2002). Foundation for Intelligent Physical Agents. (Cit. on p. 69).

FIPA Modeling: Agent Class Diagrams (2003). Geneva, Switzerland: Foundation for Iintelligent Physical Agents. (Cit. on pp. 72, 83, 84).

FIPA Modeling: Interaction Diagrams (2003). Geneva, Switzerland: Foundation for Intelligent Physical Agents. URL: http://www.auml.org/auml/documents/ID-03-07-02.pdf. (Cit. on pp. 72, 85).

Forrester, Jay Wright (1961). *Industrial Dynamics*. Productivity Press. ISBN: 0-915299-88-7. (Cit. on p. 8).

Forrester, Jay Wright (1968). *Principles of Systems*. Productivity Press. ISBN: 0-915299-87-9. (Cit. on p. 8).

Franklin, Stan and Art Graesser (1997). "Is it an Agent, or Just a Program?: A Taxonomy for Autonomous Agents". In: *ECAI '96: Proceedings of the Workshop on Intelligent Agents III, Agent Theories, Architectures, and Languages*. London, UK: Springer-Verlag, pp. 21–35. ISBN: 3-540-62507-0. (Cit. on p. 24).

Garcia, Ana Cristina Bicharra, Anderson Lopes, and Cristiana Bentes (2001). "Electronic Auction with autonomous intelligent agents: Finding opportunities by being there". In: *Inteligencia Artificial, Revista Iberoamericana de Inteligencia Artificial* 13, pp. 45–52. (Cit. on p. 17).

Genesereth, Michael R. (1991). "Knowledge Interchange Format". In: *Principles of Knowledge Representation and Reasoning: Proceedings of the 2nd International Conference*. Cambridge, MA: Morgan Kaufmann. (Cit. on p. 69).

Georgeff, Michael P. et al. (1999). "The Belief-Desire-Intention Model of Agency". In: *ATAL '98: Proceedings of the 5th International Workshop on Intelligent Agents V, Agent Theories, Architectures, and Languages*. London, UK: Springer-Verlag, pp. 1–10. ISBN: 3-540-65713-4. (Cit. on p. 52).

Giorgini, P. et al. (2004). "The Tropos Methodology: An Overview". In: *Methodologies And Software Engineering For Agent Systems*. Kluwer Academic Publishing. (Cit. on p. 92).

Glaser, Norbert (1997). "Multi-Agent Systems Methodologies and Applications". In: vol. 1286/1997. Lecture Notes in Computer Science. Springer Berlin / Heidelberg. Chap. The CoMoMAS methodology and environment for multi-agent system development, pp. 1–16. DOI: 10.1007/BFb0030077. (Cit. on pp. 86, 87).

Gomez-Sanz, Jorge J. et al. (2008). "Towards an Agent-Oriented Paradigm". In: Position Statement for FOSE-MAS. AAMAS 08. URL: http://www.cs.kuleuven.be/~danny/fose-mas/abstracts/gomez-sanz.pdf. (Cit. on p. 72).

Gopalan, N. P. and J. Akilandeswari (2005). "A distributed, fault-tolerant multi-agent web mining system for scalable web search". In: *AIC'05: Proceedings of the 5th WSEAS International Conference on Applied Informatics and Communications*. Stevens Point, Wisconsin, USA: World Scientific, Engineering Academy, and Society (WSEAS), pp. 384–390. ISBN: 960-8457-35-1. (Cit. on p. 16).

Granger, Clive W. J. (2005). "A perspective on the reliability of economic and financial predictive models". In: *Wealth*, pp. 12–13. (Cit. on p. 96).

Greenough, Chris et al. (Apr. 2010). "An Approach to the Parallelisation of Agent-Based Applications". In: *ERCIM News* 81, pp. 42–43. ISSN: 0926-4981. (Cit. on p. 99).

Guyot, Paul and Shinichi Honiden (Sept. 2006). "Agent-Based Participatory Simulations: Merging Multi-Agent Systems and Role-Playing Games". In: *Journal of Artificial Societies and Social Simulation* 9.4. URL: http://jasss.soc.surrey.ac.uk/9/4/8.html. (Cit. on p. 10).

Hackathorn, Richard (Mar. 2007). "Serious Games in Virtual Worlds: The Future of Enterprise Business Intelligence". In: *BeyeNETWORK*. URL: http://www.b-eye-network.com/view/4163. (Cit. on p. 10).

Heine, Bernd-O., Matthias Meyer, and Oliver Strangfeld (2005). "Stylised Facts and the Contribution of Simulation to the Economic Analysis of Budgeting". In: *Journal of*

Artificial Societies and Social Simulation 8, p. 4. URL: http://econpapers.repec.org/RePEc:jas:jasssj:2005-62-1. (Cit. on p. 98).

Jackson, Michael A. (1975). *Principles of Program Design*. Orlando, FL, USA: Academic Press, Inc. ISBN: 0123790506. (Cit. on pp. 128, 169).

Jung, David, Gordon Cheng, and Alexander Zelinsky (1998). "Experiments in Realising Cooperation between Autonomous Mobile Robots". In: *he Fifth International Symposium on Experimental Robotics V*. London, UK: Springer-Verlag, pp. 609–620. ISBN: 3-540-76218-3. (Cit. on pp. 29, 39).

Kakas, Antonis and Pavlos Moraitis (2003). "Argumentation based decision making for autonomous agents". In: *AAMAS '03: Proceedings of the second international joint conference on Autonomous agents and multiagent systems*. New York, NY, USA: ACM, pp. 883–890. ISBN: 1-58113-683-8. DOI: http://doi.acm.org/10.1145/860575.860717. (Cit. on p. 15).

Kendall, E.A., M.T. Malkoun, and C. Jiang (1996). "A Methodology for developing Agent Based Systems for Enterprise Integration". In: *First Australian Workshop on Distributed Artificial Intelligence*. Ed. by D.Lukose and C.Zahng. Springer-Verlag. (Cit. on p. 82).

Keyhanipour, Amir Hosein et al. (2005). "Aggregation of web search engines based on users' preferences in WebFusion". In: *AIML 05 Conference*. (Cit. on p. 16).

Kheirabadi, M.T. and H. Mohammadi (2007). "MARP: A Multi-Agent Routing Protocol for Ad-hoc Network". In: *Communications and Networking in China, 2007. CHINACOM '07*, pp. 234–238. DOI: 10.1109/CHINACOM.2007.4469371. (Cit. on p. 16).

Klügl, Franziska and Guido Rindsfüser (2007). "Multiagent System Technologies". In: Springer. Chap. Large-Scale Agent-Based Pedestrian Simulation, pp. 145–156. (Cit. on p. 17).

Kok, Jelle R. and Nikos Vlassis (2006). "Collaborative Multiagent Reinforcement Learning by Payoff Propagation". In: *Journal of Machine Learning Research* 7, pp. 1789–1828. (Cit. on p. 15).

Kok, K. et al. (2008). "Agent-Based Electricity Balancing with Distributed Energy Resources, A Multiperspective Case Study". In: *Proceedings of the 41st Annual Hawaii International Conference on System Sciences*, p. 173. DOI: 10.1109/HICSS.2008.46. (Cit. on p. 17).

LeBaron, Blake (2006). "Agent-based Computational Finance". In: *Handbook of Computational Economics*. Ed. by Leigh Tesfatsion and Kenneth L. Judd. 1st ed. Vol. 2. Elsevier. Chap. 24, pp. 1187–1233. URL: http://econpapers.repec.org/RePEc:eee:hecchp:2-24. (Cit. on p. 18).

LeBaron, Blake and Peter Winker (June 2008). "Introduction to the Special Issue on Agent-Based Models for Economic Policy Advice". In: *Journal of Economics and Statistics (Jahrbuecher fuer Nationaloekonomie und Statistik)* 228.2+3, pp. 141–148. URL: http://ideas.repec.org/a/jns/jbstat/v228y2008i2-3p141-148.html. (Cit. on p. 18).

Lehtiniemi, Tuukka (2008). "Macroeconomic Indicators in a Virtual Economy". MA thesis. Helsinki University. (Cit. on p. 10).

Lempert, Robert (2002). "Agent-Based Modeling as Organizational and Public Policy Simulators". In: *Proceedings of the National Academy of Sciences of the United States of*

America 99.10, pp. 7195–7196. ISSN: 00278424. DOI: 10.2307/3057839. URL: http://dx.doi.org/10.2307/3057839. (Cit. on p. 18).

Luo, Dan et al. (2007). "Agent and Multi-Agent Systems: Technologies and Applications". In: vol. 4496/2007. Lecture Notes in Computer Science. Berlin / Heidelberg: Springer. Chap. Building Agent Service Oriented Multi-Agent Systems, pp. 11–20. DOI: 10.1007/978-3-540-72830-6_2. (Cit. on p. 16).

Lysenko, Mikola and Roshan M. D'Souza (2008). "A Framework for Megascale Agent Based Model Simulations on Graphics Processing Units". In: *Journal of Artificial Societies and Social Simulation* 11.4, p. 10. ISSN: 1460-7425. URL: http://jasss.soc.surrey.ac.uk/11/4/10.html. (Cit. on p. 100).

Macal, Charles M. and Michael J. North (Nov. 2006). "Introduction to Agent-based Modeling and Simulation". MCS LANS Informal Seminar slides. URL: http://www.mcs.anl.gov/~leyffer/listn/slides-06/MacalNorth.pdf. (Cit. on p. 23).

Macker, J.P. et al. (2005). "Multi-agent systems in mobile ad hoc networks". In: *Military Communications Conference, 2005*. Vol. 2, pp. 883–889. DOI: 10.1109/MILCOM.2005.1605792. (Cit. on p. 16).

Macy, Michael and Yoshimichi Sato (2010). "The Surprising Success of a Replication That Failed". In: *Journal of Artificial Societies and Social Simulation* 13, p. 2. URL: http://econpapers.repec.org/RePEc:jas:jasssj:2010-15-1. (Cit. on p. 98).

Maes, Pattie (1991). "The agent network architecture (ANA)". In: *SIGART Bull.* 2.4, pp. 115–120. ISSN: 0163-5719. DOI: http://doi.acm.org/10.1145/122344.122367. (Cit. on pp. 27, 29, 36).

Makridakis, Spyros, Robin M. Hogarth, and Anil Gaba (2010). "Why Forecasts Fail. What to Do Instead". In: *MIT Sloan Management Review*. (Cit. on p. 96).

Manvi, S. S. and M. S. Kakkasageri (2008). "Multicast routing in mobile ad hoc networks by using a multiagent system". In: *Inf. Sci.* 178.6, pp. 1611–1628. ISSN: 0020-0255. DOI: http://dx.doi.org/10.1016/j.ins.2007.11.005. (Cit. on p. 16).

Martínez, José-F et al. (2007). "An approach for applying multi-agent technology into wireless sensor networks". In: *EATIS '07: Proceedings of the 2007 Euro American conference on Telematics and information systems*. New York, NY, USA: ACM, pp. 1–8. ISBN: 978-1-59593-598-4. DOI: http://doi.acm.org/10.1145/1352694.1352717. (Cit. on p. 16).

Metropolis, Nicholas and Stanislaw Ulam (Sept. 1949). "The Monte Carlo Method". In: *Journal of the American Statistical Association* 44.247, pp. 335–341. (Cit. on p. 5).

Meyer, Matthias, Iris Lorscheid, and Klaus G. Troitzsch (2009). "The Development of Social Simulation as Reflected in the First Ten Years of JASSS: a Citation and Co-Citation Analysis". In: *Journal of Artificial Societies and Social Simulation* 12. URL: http://ideas.repec.org/a/jas/jasssj/2009-47-2.html. (Cit. on p. 95).

Minkel, J.R. (Feb. 2008). *Robotics Prof Sees Threat in Military Robots*. URL: http://www.sciam.com/article.cfm?id=robotics-prof-sees-threat-in-robots. (Cit. on p. 31).

Mobile Agent System Interoperability Facilities Specification (1997). Boston. URL: http://www.omg.org/cgi-bin/doc?orbos/97-10-05. (Cit. on p. 184).

Morley, David and Karen Myers (2004). "The SPARK Agent Framework". In: *AAMAS '04: Proceedings of the Third International Joint Conference on Autonomous Agents and Multiagent Systems*. Washington, DC, USA: IEEE Computer Society, pp. 714–721. ISBN: 1-58113-864-4. DOI: http://dx.doi.org/10.1109/AAMAS.2004.267. (Cit. on p. 181).

Mumcu, Ayse and Ismail Saglam (2008). "Marriage Formation/Dissolution and Marital Distribution in a Two-Period Economic Model of Matching with Cooperative Bargaining". In: *Journal of Artificial Societies and Social Simulation* 11. URL: http://ideas.repec.org/a/jas/jasssj/2007-85-6.html. (Cit. on p. 19).

Munoz-Salinas, Rafael et al. (2005). "A multi-agent system architecture for mobile robot navigation based on fuzzy and visual behaviour". In: *Robotica* 23.6, pp. 689–699. ISSN: 0263-5747. DOI: http://dx.doi.org/10.1017/S0263574704001390. (Cit. on p. 14).

Nakashima, Hideyuki and Itsuki Noda (1998). "Dynamic Subsumption Architecture for Programming Intelligent Agents". In: *ICMAS '98: Proceedings of the 3rd International Conference on Multi Agent Systems*. Washington, DC, USA: IEEE Computer Society, p. 190. ISBN: 0-8186-8500-X. (Cit. on p. 34).

Neumann, John von (1966). *Theory of Self-Reproducing Automata*. Ed. by Arthur W. Burks. Champaign, IL, USA: University of Illinois Press. ISBN: 0-598-37798-0. (Cit. on p. 9).

Nguyen, G.T. et al. (June 2002). *Agent Platform Evaluation and Comparison*. Tech. rep. Pellucid 5FP IST-2001-34519. Institute of Informatics, Slovak academy of sciences. (Cit. on p. 175).

Niimi, Ayahiko and Osamu Konishi (2004). "Knowledge-Based Intelligent Information and Engineering Systems". In: vol. 3215/2004. Lecture Notes in Computer Science. Berlin / Heidelberg: Springer. Chap. Extension of Multiagent Data Mining for Distributed Databases, pp. 780–787. DOI: 10.1007/b100916. (Cit. on p. 16).

Nikolai, Cynthia and Gregory Madey (2009). "Tools of the Trade: A Survey of Various Agent Based Modeling Platforms". In: *Journal of Artificial Societies and Social Simulation* 12.2, p. 2. ISSN: 1460-7425. URL: http://jasss.soc.surrey.ac.uk/12/2/2.html. (Cit. on p. 175).

North, M. J. et al. (Jan. 2008). "Agent-based modeling and simulation for EXASCALE computing". In: *SciDAC Rev.* 8, pp. 34–41. (Cit. on pp. 99, 186).

nVidia GPU Programming Guide (2005). nVidia. (Cit. on p. 100).

Nwana, Hyacinth S. (Sept. 1996). "Software Agents: An Overview". In: *Knowledge Engineering Review* 11.3, pp. 1–40. (Cit. on pp. 28, 38, 58, 61).

Odell, James (2003). *Agent UML: What is It and Why Do I Care*. URL: http://www.jamesodell.com/What-is-UML.pdf. (Cit. on p. 75).

Ohdaira, Tetsushi and Takao Terano (2009). "Cooperation in the Prisoner's Dilemma Game Based on the Second-Best Decision". In: *Journal of Artificial Societies and Social Simulation* 12, p. 4. URL: http://econpapers.repec.org/RePEc:jas:jasssj:2008-7-4. (Cit. on p. 18).

OMG Unified Modeling LanguageTM (OMG UML), Superstructure (Feb. 2009). Object Management Group. (Cit. on pp. 138, 154, 157).

Ormerod, Paul and Bridget Rosewell (2009). "Validation and Verification of Agent-Based Models in the Social Sciences". In: pp. 130–140. DOI: http://dx.doi.org/10. 1007/978-3-642-01109-2_10. (Cit. on p. 98).

Parunak, H. Van Dyke and James Odell (2001). "Representing social structures in UML". In: AGENTS '01: Proceedings of the fifth international conference on Autonomous agents. New York, NY, USA: ACM, pp. 100–101. ISBN: 1-58113-326-X. DOI: http://doi. acm.org/10.1145/375735.376008. (Cit. on p. 72).

Pechoucek, Michal and David Sislak (2009). "Agent-Based Approach to Free-Flight Planning, Control, and Simulation". In: IEEE Intelligent Systems 24.1, pp. 14–17. URL: http://www2.computer.org/portal/web/csdl/doi/10.1109/MIS. 2009.1. (Cit. on p. 17).

Pell, Barney et al. (1998). "An autonomous spacecraft agent prototype". In: Autonomous Robots. ACM Press, pp. 253–261. (Cit. on p. 15).

Perdikeas, Menelaos K., Fotis G. Chatzipapadopoulos, and Iakovos S. Venieris (1999). "An Evaluation Study of Mobile Agent Technology: Standardization, Implementation and Evolution". In: ICMCS '99: Proceedings of the IEEE International Conference on Multimedia Computing and Systems. Washington, DC, USA: IEEE Computer Society, p. 287. ISBN: 0-7695-0253-9. (Cit. on p. 175).

Peysakhov, Maxim et al. (2006). "Quorum sensing on mobile ad-hoc networks". In: AAMAS '06: Proceedings of the fifth international joint conference on Autonomous agents and multiagent systems. New York, NY, USA: ACM, pp. 1104–1106. ISBN: 1-59593-303-4. DOI: http://doi.acm.org/10.1145/1160633.1160831. (Cit. on p. 16).

Ping, Yi et al. (2008). "Distributed intrusion detection for mobile ad hoc networks". In: Journal of Systems Engineering and Electronics 19.4, pp. 851–859. ISSN: 1004-4132. DOI: DOI : 10 . 1016 / S1004 - 4132(08) 60163 - 2. URL: http : / / www . sciencedirect . com / science / article / B82XK - 4T9VN1S - 14 / 2 / 08b182bf7e67db67fdfc03302bd3b536. (Cit. on p. 16).

Popper, Karl R. (1998). Logik der Forschung. Mohr. (Cit. on p. 98).

Rao, Anand S. (1996). "AgentSpeak(L): BDI agents speak out in a logical computable language". In: MAAMAW '96: Proceedings of the 7th European workshop on Modelling autonomous agents in a multi-agent world : agents breaking away. Secaucus, NJ, USA: Springer-Verlag New York, Inc., pp. 42–55. ISBN: 3-540-60852-4. (Cit. on pp. 15, 54).

Rauhut, Heiko and Marcel Junker (2009). "Punishment Deters Crime Because Humans Are Bounded in Their Strategic Decision-Making". In: Journal of Artificial Societies and Social Simulation 12, p. 3. URL: http://econpapers.repec.org/RePEc:jas: jasssj:2008-82-2. (Cit. on p. 19).

Robison-Cox, James F., Richard F. Martell, and Cynthia G. Emrich (2007). "Simulating Gender Stratification". In: Journal of Artificial Societies and Social Simulation 10, p. 3. URL: http://econpapers.repec.org/RePEc:jas:jasssj:2006-72-2. (Cit. on p. 18).

Royce, Winston W. (Aug. 1970). "Managing the Development of Large Software Systems". In: Proc. IEEE Wescon, pp. 1–9. (Cit. on p. 106).

Russell, Stuart and Peter Norvig (1995). *Artificial Intelligence: A Modern Approach.* Englewood Cliffs, New Jersey: Prentice Hall. ISBN: 0-13-103805-2. (Cit. on pp. 21, 28, 40, 43).

Řepa, Václav (1999). *Analýza a návrh informačních systémů.* Ekopress. ISBN: 80-86119-13-0. (Cit. on pp. 104, 128).

Sabar, M., B. Montreuil, and J. M. Frayret (2009). "A multi-agent-based approach for personnel scheduling in assembly centers". In: *Eng. Appl. Artif. Intell.* 22.7, pp. 1080–1088. ISSN: 0952-1976. DOI: http://dx.doi.org/10.1016/j.engappai.2009.02.009. (Cit. on p. 18).

Sallila, Seppo (2010). "Using Microsimulation to Optimize an Income Transfer System Towards Poverty Reduction". In: *Journal of Artificial Societies and Social Simulation* 13. URL: http://ideas.repec.org/a/jas/jasssj/2008-2-3.html. (Cit. on p. 18).

Sandholm, Tuomas W. (1999). "Distributed rational decision making". In: pp. 201–258. (Cit. on p. 66).

Schreiber, Guus et al. (1994). "CommonKADS: A Comprehensive Methodology for KBS Development". In: *IEEE Expert* 9.6, pp. 28–37. (Cit. on p. 86).

Schutte, Sebastian (2010). "Optimization and Falsification in Empirical Agent-Based Models". In: *Journal of Artificial Societies and Social Simulation* 13, p. 1. URL: http://econpapers.repec.org/RePEc:jas:jasssj:2009-30-2. (Cit. on p. 98).

Shafiq, M. Omair, Ying Ding, and Dieter Fensel (2006). "Bridging Multi Agent Systems and Web Services: towards interoperability between Software Agents and Semantic Web Services". In: *EDOC '06: Proceedings of the 10th IEEE International Enterprise Distributed Object Computing Conference.* Washington, DC, USA: IEEE Computer Society, pp. 85–96. ISBN: 0-7695-2558-X. DOI: http://dx.doi.org/10.1109/EDOC.2006.18. (Cit. on p. 16).

Shoham, Yoav (1993). "Agent-oriented programming". In: *Artificial Intelligence* 60.1, pp. 51–92. ISSN: 0004-3702. DOI: http://dx.doi.org/10.1016/0004-3702(93)90034-9. (Cit. on pp. 69, 71, 75).

— (1991). "AGENT0: A Simple Agent Language and Its Interpreter". In: *Proceedings of the Ninth National Conference on Artificial Intelligence.* AAAI Press, Menlo Park, CA, pp. 704–709. URL: http://jmvidal.cse.sc.edu/library/shoham91a.pdf. (Cit. on p. 15).

Shoham, Yoav and Kevin Leyton-Brown (2009). *Multiagent Systems: Algorithmic, Game-Theoretic, and Logical Foundations.* New York: Cambridge University Press. ISBN: 978-0-521-89943-7. (Cit. on p. 39).

Shukri, S. R. Mohd and M. K. Mohd Shaukhi (2008). "A Study on Multi-Agent Behavior in a Soccer Game Domain". In: *Proceedings of World Academy of Science, Engineering and Technology* 28, pp. 308–312. ISSN: 2070-3740. URL: http://www.waset.org/pwaset/v28/v28-55.pdf. (Cit. on p. 15).

Sichman, J.S. et al. (1994). "A social reasoning mechanism based on dependence networks". In: *Proceeedings of the Eleventh European Conference on Artificial Intelligence.* Ed. by A.G. Cohn. John Wiley & Sons, pp. 188–192. (Cit. on p. 65).

Soukupová, Jana et al. (2003). *Mikroekonomie*. 3rd ed. Management Press. ISBN: 80-7261-061-9. (Cit. on p. 42).

Stroud, Phillip et al. (2007). "Spatial Dynamics of Pandemic Influenza in a Massive Artificial Society". In: *Journal of Artificial Societies and Social Simulation* 10. URL: http: //ideas.repec.org/a/jas/jasssj/2007-34-2.html. (Cit. on pp. 17, 100, 186).

Šalamon, Tomáš (2009). "A Three-Layer Approach to Testing of Multi-agent Systems". In: *Information Systems Development: Towards a Service Provision Society*. Ed. by George Angelos Papadopoulos et al. Springer US, pp. 393–401. DOI: 10.1007/b137171. (Cit. on p. 134).

— (2008a). "Evaluation of Effects of Investment Incentives Using Simulation in a Multi-agent System". In: *Proceedings from Fourth International Bata Conference*. (Cit. on p. 18).

— (2008b). "Zvládání složitosti multiagentního systému". In: *Sborník prací účastníků vědeckého semináře doktorského studia*. Ed. by Jakub Fischer. FIS VŠE, pp. 60–68. (Cit. on p. 99).

Šišlák, David, Přemysl Volf, and Michal Pěchouček (2010). "Large-scale Agent-based Simulation of Air-traffic". In: *Proceedings of the Twentieth European Meeting on Cybernetics and Systems Research*. ISBN: 9783852061788. (Cit. on p. 100).

Tesfatsion, Leigh (2002). *Agent-Based Computational Economics: Growing Economies from the Bottom Up*. ISU Economics Working Paper 1. Iowa State University. (Cit. on pp. 6, 8).

Tian, Jiang and Huaglory Tianfield (2007). "Advanced Intelligent Computing Theories and Applications. With Aspects of Theoretical and Methodological Issues". In: vol. 4681/2007. Lecture Notes in Computer Science. Berlin / Heidelberg: Springer. Chap. Multi-agent Based Dynamic Supply Chain Formation in Semi-monopolized Circumstance, pp. 179–189. DOI: 10.1007/978-3-540-74171-8_18. (Cit. on p. 17).

Tumer, Kagan and Adrian Agogino (2007). "Distributed agent-based air traffic flow management". In: *AAMAS '07: Proceedings of the 6th international joint conference on Autonomous agents and multiagent systems*. New York, NY, USA: ACM, pp. 1–8. ISBN: 978-81-904262-7-5. DOI: http://doi.acm.org/10.1145/1329125.1329434. (Cit. on p. 17).

Ustun, Volkan, Levent Yilmaz, and Jeffrey S. Smith (2006). "A conceptual model for agent-based simulation of physical security systems". In: *ACM-SE 44: Proceedings of the 44th annual Southeast regional conference*. New York, NY, USA: ACM, pp. 365–370. ISBN: 1-59593-315-8. DOI: http://doi.acm.org/10.1145/1185448.1185530. (Cit. on p. 18).

Vecchiola, C. et al. (2003). "An Agent Oriented Programming Language Targeting the Microsoft Common Language Runtime". In: *1st Int.Workshop on C and .NET Technologies on Algorithms, Computer Graphics, Visualization, Computer Vision and Distributed Computing*. (Cit. on p. 15).

Vidal, José M. (2006). "Fundamentals of Multiagent Systems with NetLogo Examples". e-textbook. (Cit. on pp. 39, 40, 43).

Wadhwa, Subhash and Bibhushan Bibhushan (2006). "Supply chain modeling: The agent based approach". In: *Information Control Problems in Manufacturing*. Ed. by Alexandre

Dolgui, Gérard Morel, and Carlos Pereira. Vol. 12. DOI: 10.3182/20060517-3-US-00247. (Cit. on p. 18).

Wagner, Gerd (2003). "The agent-object-relationship metamodel: towards a unified view of state and behavior". In: *Inf. Syst.* 28.5, pp. 475–504. ISSN: 0306-4379. DOI: http://dx.doi.org/10.1016/S0306-4379(02)00027-3. (Cit. on p. 76).

Wang, Yongwei et al. (2009). "Cluster based partitioning for agent-based crowd simulations". In: *Proceedings of the 2009 Winter Simulation Conference.* (Cit. on p. 100).

"Multiagent Systems: A Modern Approach to Distributed Modern Approach to Artificial Intelligence" (1999). In: ed. by Gerhard Weiss. Cambridge, Massachusetts: MIT Press. ISBN: 0-262-23203-0. (Cit. on p. 15).

Wilensky, Uri and William Rand (2007). "Making Models Match: Replicating an Agent-Based Model". In: *Journal of Artificial Societies and Social Simulation* 10. URL: http://ideas.repec.org/a/jas/jasssj/2007-7-2.html. (Cit. on p. 98).

Winikoff, Michael and Lin Padgham (July 2004). "Methodologies and Software Engineering for Agent Systems. The Agent-Oriented Software Engineering handbook." In: ed. by Marie-Pierre Gleizes Federico Bergenti and Franco Zambonelli. Kluwer Publishing. Chap. The Prometheus Methodology, pp. 217–234. (Cit. on pp. 91, 92, 104).

Wnuk, Kamil, Brian Fulkerson, and Jeremi Sudol (2006). "A Multi Agent Approach to Vision Based Robot Scavenging". In: *Proceedings of the National Conference on Artificial Intelligence.* (Cit. on p. 15).

Wooldridge, Michael (2002). *An introduction to multiagent systems.* Chichester: John Wiley & Sons. ISBN: 0-471-49691-X. (Cit. on pp. 9, 25, 38, 41, 46, 47, 52–54, 60, 61).

— (2000). *Reasoning about Rational Agents.* Cambridge, Massachusetts: The MIT Press. (Cit. on pp. 52, 53).

Wooldridge, Michael and Nicholas R. Jennings (1995). "Intelligent Agents: Theory and Practice". In: *Knowledge Engineering Review* 10.2, pp. 115–152. (Cit. on p. 23).

Wooldridge, Michael, Nicholas R. Jennings, and David Kinny (2000). "The Gaia Methodology for Agent-Oriented Analysis and Design". In: *Autonomous Agents and Multi-Agent Systems* 3.3, pp. 285–312. ISSN: 1387-2532. DOI: http://dx.doi.org/10.1023/A:1010071910869. (Cit. on pp. 87, 88).

Yamamoto, Gaku, Hideki Tai, and Hideyuki Mizuta (2007). "A platform for massive agent-based simulation and its evaluation". In: *AAMAS '07: Proceedings of the 6th international joint conference on Autonomous agents and multiagent systems.* New York, NY, USA: ACM, pp. 1–3. ISBN: 978-81-904262-7-5. DOI: http://doi.acm.org/10.1145/1329125.1329288. (Cit. on p. 99).

Zadeh, Lofti A. (1988). "Fuzzy Logic". In: *Computer* 21.4, pp. 83–93. ISSN: 0018-9162. DOI: http://doi.ieeecomputersociety.org/10.1109/2.53. (Cit. on p. 50).

Zhong, Wei and Yushim Kim (2010). "Using Model Replication to Improve the Reliability of Agent-Based Models". In: *SBP*, pp. 118–127. (Cit. on p. 98).

Zhu, Hong and Lijun Shan (2005). "Agent-Oriented Modelling and Specification of Web Services". In: *WORDS '05: Proceedings of the 10th IEEE International Workshop on Object-Oriented Real-Time Dependable Systems.* Washington, DC, USA: IEEE Com-

puter Society, pp. 152–159. ISBN: 0-7695-2347-1. DOI: http://dx.doi.org/10.
1109/WORDS.2005.14. (Cit. on p. 16).

Index

3APL, 15

Abstraction, 22, 74
Accessible environment, 21
Achievement goal, 55
Action, 24, 73, 126, 139, 152
Action function, 41, 47
Activation level, 36
Activity diagram, 84, 112, 116, 117, 119,
        124, 163
Add-list, 36
Agent, 13
    approach, 121, 174
    architecture, 60
    behavior-based, 29
    characteristics, 26
    class, 76, 115, 125, 139
    communication, 69, 115
    communication language, 69
    deliberative, 27, 40
    features, 78
    framework, 124
    goal-based, 40
    hybrid, 29
    interactions, 63
    natural, 23
    network architecture, 36

paradigm, 69
physical, 23
purely reactive, 29
reaction, 34
reactive, 27, 29
software, 23
specification, 174
type, 76
utility-based, 40
Agent class diagram, 83
Agent Class Diagram Superstructure
        Meta-model, 83
Agent conceptual modeling, 137
Agent diagram, 115, 119, 125
    detailed, 144
    global, 138
Agent Oriented Methodology for
        Enterprise Modeling, 82
Agent-based
    modeling, 8
    modeling software, 173
    simulations, 38
Agent-oriented
    methodologies, 81
    programming, 54, 71, 124, 138
Agent0, 15
Agentology, 103, 169

University of Birmingham, 187
University of Michigan, 187
University of Minnsota, 187
Universität Osnabrück, 187
UPMS, 82
Use case, 82, 109
User environment, 117
User interface, 122, 126, 129
Utility, 42
    cardinal, 42
    expected, 43
    function, 43
    maximization, 43

net, 44
ordinal, 42
Utility-based agents, 40
Utility-based approach, 42

Virtual economy, 10
Virtual world, 10
Visualization, 122

Waterfall approach, 106
Web services, 16

Zero-sum games, 67

Lightning Source UK Ltd.
Milton Keynes UK
UKOW051802190412

191087UK00003B/17/P